TO
BILL MENEES

Who died of cancer on his fifty-fourth birthday. He was a dear and esteemed friend. He was a true Christian. Bill gave me much encouragement in the ministry when I was on the "Hill Difficulty." I miss him very much.

> *"Precious in the sight of the LORD is the death of his saints."*
>
> Psalm 116:15

ACKNOWLEDGMENTS
AND THANKS

To Veronica Owens, my secretary, for all the typing, typing, and retyping; for all the extra hours she spent on the manuscript and for her words of encouragement to complete the book.

To Pastor Walter Chantry, for the help and encouragement to have it published.

To Pastor Albert Martin, for the many of his sermons that supplied some of the material.

To the den Dulk Foundation, for financial assistance.

To the wife of my youth for her patience.

From John Bunyan's "Author's Apology" in respect to "Pilgrim's Progress":

Thus I set Pen to Paper with delight,
   And quickly had my thoughts in black and white.
For having now my Method by the end,
   Still as I pull'd, it came; and so I penn'd
It down; until it came at last to be
   For length and breadth, the bigness which you see.
Well, when I had thus put mine ends together,
   I shew'd them others, that I might see whether
They would condemn them, or them justify:
   And some said, let them live; some, let them die;
Some said, John, print it; others said, Not so.
   Some said, It might do good, others said, No.
Now as I in a straight, and did not see
   Which was the best thing to be done by me:
At last I thought, Since ye are thus divided,
   I print it will; and so the case decided,
For, thought I, Some, I see, would have it done,
   Though others in that Channel do not run:
To prove then who advised for the best,
   Thus I thought fit to put it to the test.
I further thought, if now I did deny
   Those that would have it thus, to gratifie;
I did not know but hinder them I might
   Of that which would to them be great delight.
For those that were not for its coming forth,
   I said to them, Offend you, I am loth
Yet since your Brethren pleased with it be,

Forbear to judge, till you do further see.
If that thou wilt not read, let it alone;
  Some love the meat, some love to pick the bone:
Yea, that I might them better palliate,
  I did too with them thus Expostulate:
May I not write in such a stile as this?
  In such a method too, and yet not miss
Mine end thy good? why may it not be done?
  Dark Clouds bring Waters, when the bright bring none.

TABLE OF CONTENTS

FOREWORD

This book has its roots in an unceasing burden to see biblical evangelism restored to the church and to see a proper relationship established between sound doctrine and true heavenly zeal in evangelism.

We must always be willing to examine ourselves by the Scriptures and church history. If we compare the evangelistic labors of the apostles, the Reformers and many other esteemed men who were used in evangelism, such as Bunyan, Whitefield, Edwards and Spurgeon, with the present-day evangelism, we will soon see there is a great difference in respect to the message and methods. Anyone who will make an honest comparison will soon see a vast difference in the message in many areas, but particularly in respect to the character of God, the condition of unregenerate men, the biblical doctrine of regeneration, the Spirit's effectual calling of sinners to Christ, the person and work of Christ as it relates to redemption accomplished and applied, and the relationship of the Ten Commandments to gospel proclamation. The question that must be foremost in such an examination is, Which is more biblical?

This book is written not because we do not have sufficient material on the subject of evangelism, but because most of the material is on methods, or to stir up zeal for evangelism, and there is very little on any sort of biblical examination of the message and methods.

The true servant of Christ, because he is one under the authority of God's Word, will always be seeking to conform his life, practice, and preaching more closely to the Bible.

Church history teaches us that the church is always drifting away from the Scriptures — always in need of self-examination and reviving. One of the main purposes of this book is to plead for such an examination in the area of evangelism in respect to the biblical content of the message and the biblical foundation for many of the methods employed in evangelism. It is not an idle question to ask, Do present-day evangelistic practices conform to the teaching of the Word of God? Timothy was told to "do the work of an evangelist." Well, what did he do? How did he go about it? You can study Paul's Epistles to him in vain to find anything like what we have on our contemporary scene.

There is no question that there is some truth in modern evangelism or no one would be saved, but people are saved by the truth, not the mixture of error.

The other question that needs to be asked is, How many are deceived and misled by unbiblical messages and unbiblical methods? To put the question another way, How many have been spiritually butchered by unbiblical evangelism?

Since worship and witness are the two main functions of the Christian church, evangelism is a good work, but it must be done by a *right rule* — the Word of God. It must have a *right end in view* — the glory of God and the salvation of sinners. And it must be carried on with a *right motive* — love to God and concern for His glory, and love to man and concern for his good.

An examination of our evangelism will do no harm. The particular areas of examination this book deals with are in respect to the biblical teachings on:

1. The condition of man.
2. The Person and work of Christ.
3. The accomplishment and application of the work of Christ on the cross.

4. The place of the law in the proclamation of the gospel.

This book does not claim to be balanced in every area of evangelism. It is not dealing so much with the means that God uses in converting sinners as with the cause. It is dealing more with the Godward side than with man's responsibility to evangelize. There is much more emphasis on the sovereignty of God than on human responsibility, because that is one of the weak links in modern evangelism. There is much more space given to the biblical teaching on election than to the responsibility of the elect, again, because election is almost the lost doctrine of the Bible in most modern evangelism, though it is the doctrine that guarantees the success of evangelism.

There will be more emphasis on Christian doctrine only because there is a vital relationship between true biblical evangelism and sound doctrine. When the message now being delivered in the evangelistic efforts is scrutinized by Holy Writ, it is found wanting — lacking in that which is vital to a genuine conversion; lacking in what is essential if sinners are to be shown their need of a Savior; lacking in that which will produce transformed lives.

This book is not written with a censorious spirit seeking to make men offenders for a word, nor is it that we look for perfection and complain because we cannot find it; nor that we criticize others because they are not doing things as we think they should be done. No! It is a matter far more serious than that. Most of the evangelism of our day is not only superficial; it is radically defective in the message and methods.

Just as the world was not ready for the New Testament before it received the Old, and just as the Jews were not prepared for the ministry of Christ until John the Baptist had gone before Him with his clear call to repentance, so the unsaved are in no condition today for the gospel until the law is applied to their hearts, ". . . for by the *law* is the knowledge of sin" (Rom. 3:20). It is a waste of time to sow seeds on ground that has never been plowed. What the unconverted need to hear about is the character of Him with whom they have to do — His claims on them, His righteous demands, and the infinite consequences of disregarding Him and going their own way. Since Christ is a Savior from sin, it is imperative to know what sin is. The very first thing said about Him in the New Testament is, " . . . thou shalt call his name *Jesus*: for he shall save his people from their *sins*" (Matt. 1:21) — not from life's casualties, or life's problems, or life's disappointments, or just the consequences of sin, but from *sin*.

Repentance is necessary to salvation. Jesus said, ". . . except ye repent, ye shall *all* likewise perish" (Luke 13:3). Repentance is just as essential as faith; in fact, the latter cannot be without the former. Since repentance is another weak link in modern evangelism, we have given much more consideration to this aspect of the message of evangelism.

This book is about the biblical view and practice of evangelism with the emphasis on the areas that are weak or missing in most modern evangelism. And again, I want to be very clear on the chief motive for this book, that is, to provoke serious thought about the message and methods of modern evangelism, which I trust will lead to a biblical examination of both. The methods grow out of the message — and the message stems from theology.

This book is not for you if you are not willing to have your thinking on this subject challenged or your message and methods examined. If, on the other hand, you are willing to open your Bible and examine every assertion made in this book and seek a biblical answer to the questions raised, this book will provide some provocative thoughts on the subject of evangelism and be the means of restoring a more biblical and God-centered evangelism.

INTRODUCTION:
EVANGELIZE OR FOSSILIZE

The church that does not evangelize will fossilize, that is, dry up and become useless to Christ and the world.

Most evangelical church leaders would agree that evangelism is of paramount importance. Others who are not evangelical agree that evangelism is important. The Roman Catholic Church believes in evangelism; the Mormons believe in evangelism (that is why they are at your door); the Jehovah's Witnesses believe in evangelism. All the cults seek converts, and they all have some success in gaining converts. There is no end to conventions, congresses or committees on evangelism.

Our differences are not that we all do not believe that the Bible teaches evangelism. Our differences lie in three main areas:

1. The *message* of evangelism — there is much disagreement on this point.
2. The *methods* of evangelism — they differ from the mass-meeting type crusades, the Mormon and Jehovah's Witnesses door-to-door method, the Campus Crusade "Four Spiritual Laws" approach, and the "revival" meeting approach.
3. The *motive* of evangelism — this also seems to be quite different. Some seem to be satisfied with statistics, just some more names added to their membership rolls.

I am not going to try to examine or evaluate all the evangelistic messages and methods, and of course, no human can go into motives. I wish to stay with evangelism among evangelicals. We have differences enough among this group.

Some of the questions that need to be asked are:

1. What about the caliber of the supposed converts?
2. Is there evidence of a real conversion experience?
3. Has there been a real conversion experience?
4. Has this conversion led to a new life in Christ, to a new purpose for living, and a new pathway of obedience?
5. Are these supposed converts brought into a living relationship with the Son of God?
6. Are they led to worship Him and serve Him in His church?

A few years ago I was asked by a pastor friend to join in with his church for a campaign with one of those "bell-ringing, horn-tooting" evangelists who conducts a kind of religious circus. But, because of some biblical and theological views, I could not compromise my convictions. My pastor friend went on with this campaign (or whatever it was). It lasted eight days, and there were 68 supposed conversions. The pastor later told me that he understood why I could not participate because in less than one month, he could not find one of the "converts." This kind of result puzzles the church leaders, or at least it should. It also puts many questions into the minds of non-Christians, such as, Is there anything to conversion?

The "follow-up programs" do not do much, because as a rule there is nothing to follow up, no reality in the beginning. It is also a little hard to develop a follow-up program from the New Testament, because when the New Testament sinners were converted, there was no need for a "follow-up program." They became followers of Christ; in other words, *they* did the following. Now, if any one thing should make us willing to examine our evangelism, it is the caliber of the supposed converts that have filled the rolls of our churches.

I want to invite you to the New Testament — to the lips and words of our Lord to examine our commission to evangelize, or, I could call it "The Heavenly Mandate" — as we find it in the following passages:

> And when they saw him, they worshipped Him: but some doubted. And Jesus came and spake unto them, saying, All power is given unto me in heaven and in earth. Go ye therefore, and make disciples of all nations, baptizing them in the name of the Father, and of the Son, and of the Holy Ghost: Teaching them to observe all things whatsoever I have commanded you: and, lo, I am with you alway, even unto the end of the world. Amen (Matt. 28:17–20).

> And he said unto them, Go ye into all the world, and preach the gospel to every creature. He that believeth and is baptized shall be saved; but he that believeth not shall be damned (Mark 16:15, 16).

> And [he] said unto them, Thus it is written, and thus it behoved Christ to suffer, and to rise from the dead the third day: and that repentance and remission of sins should be preached in his name among all nations, beginning at Jerusalem. And ye are witnesses of these things (Luke 24:46–48).

> Then said Jesus to them again, Peace be unto you: as my Father hath sent me, even so send I you (John 20:21).

> But ye shall receive power, after that the Holy Ghost is come upon you: and ye shall be witnesses unto me both in Jerusalem, and in all Judaea, and in Samaria, and unto the uttermost part of the earth (Acts 1:8).

I say again, we must evangelize or fossilize. We will,

therefore, be looking at the mandate as it is found in the above Scriptures, and we will be considering the message and the methods as they are found in the New Testament.

I will seek to set before you the difference between God-centered evangelism (which is the only biblical evangelism) and much of the man-centered evangelism. Biblical, God-centered evangelism was never more urgent than it is today. Therefore, my motive will be to encourage God-centered evangelism, to raise some questions about much of the present-day, man-centered evangelism, and to plead for the Scriptures to be the court of appeal.

EVANGELIZE

Give us a watchword for the hour,
A thrilling word, a word of power;
A battle-cry, a flaming breath
That calls to conquest or to death;
A word to rouse the Church from rest
To heed her Master's high behest—
The call is given: "Ye host arise!
Our watchword is "EVANGELIZE!"

The glad evangel now proclaim
Through all the earth in Jesus' name;
The word is ringing through the skies:
"EVANGELIZE! EVANGELIZE!"
To dying men, a fallen race,
Make known God's wondrous saving grace;
The world that now in darkness lies,
"EVANGELIZE! EVANGELIZE!"

1. EVANGELISM—WHAT IS IT?

Evangelism is the communication of a divinely inspired message that we call the gospel. It is a *message* that is definable in words, but must be communicated in word and power. "For our gospel came not unto you in word only, but also in *power*, and in the Holy Ghost, and in much assurance . . ." (I Thess. 1:5). That *message* begins with information and includes explanation, application and invitation.

The *information* is how God, our Creator and Judge, in mercy, made His Son a perfect, able and willing Savior of sinners. The *invitation* is God's summons to mankind to come to that Savior in faith and repentance, and find forgiveness, life and peace.

> And this is his commandment, that we should believe on the name of his Son Jesus Christ, and love one another, as he gave us commandment (I John 3:23).

> Jesus answered and said unto them, this is the work of God, that ye believe on him whom he hath sent (John 6:29).

The *definition* of evangelize is as follows: "To present Jesus Christ to sinful men, in order that they may come to put their trust in God, through Him to receive Him as their Saviour and serve Him as their King in the fellowship of His church."[1] You will notice that this definition is more than

---

*[1] J. I. Packer, *Evangelism and The Sovereignty of God* (Downers Grove: InterVarsity Press). This book is highly recommended.

"winning souls," or saving people from hell, or saving them from their personal problems, or from life's casualties, and you will notice that the definition includes serving Christ in His church. Much present-day evangelism would not fit this definition.

EVANGELISM IS A GOOD WORK

We want to consider evangelism as a good work, and we must ask, What determines a good work? There are three things that determine if a work is a good work.

First, a good work must be done by a *right rule*, and in the case of evangelism, that rule is the Word of God. We must examine all we do and say in evangelism by the Word of God. That is going to be shocking and revealing, but, this will be our only appeal — the Word of God. The question is not going to be, "Does it work?" but, *"Is it true?" — "Is it biblical?"* The Jehovah's Witnesses' system works because they get converts, but, is it true?

Second, a good work must have a *right end in view.* What is that end? The glory of God! God's grace, mercy, and power will be glorified in the salvation of souls, or, His righteousness, holiness, and justice will be glorified in the damnation of ungodly rejectors of His revelation. Therefore, our job is to be true to the message of evangelism, regardless of the results.

When a preacher or a church tries to effect that which only God can effect, it has shifted from God-centered evangelism to man-centered evangelism. Therefore, the end we must have in view in God-centered evangelism must be first and foremost, the glory of God. If our end is only man, then our evangelism will soon become man-centered, which represents most modern evangelism.

Third, a good work must have a *right motive.* What is the right motive in God-centered evangelism? There are two proper motives:

2

1. Love to God and concern for His glory.
2. Love to man and concern for his good.

Both of these motives spring from the Ten Commandments. Let me explain what I mean. When Jesus was asked by the lawyer, "Master, which is the great commandment in the law?" Jesus said unto him, "Thou shalt love the Lord thy God with all thy heart, and with all thy soul, and with all thy mind. This is the first and great commandment. And the second is like unto it, Thou shalt love thy neighbour as thyself. On these two commandments hang all the law and the prophets" (Matt. 22:36–40). Here our Lord gave a summary of the Ten Commandments.

Now, I said our motive for the good work of God-centered evangelism must be (1) love to God and concern for His glory, and (2) love to man and concern for his good. Well, how do we glorify God?

We glorify God by doing His will — and it is His will that we spread His name and His message of His salvation. Jesus said He glorified the Father by finishing the work that the Father gave Him to do: "I have glorified thee on the earth: I have finished *the work* which thou gavest me to do" (John 17:4).

He has given us the work of taking His message to all the world, thus our first motive must be love to God and concern for His glory. This is expressed in obedience to His revealed will. Therefore, if we are obedient to spreading God's message, He will be glorified regardless of the results. The results are past our reach, past our ability, and, thank God, past our responsibility.

Our second motive — love to man and concern for his good — again springs from our Lord's summary of the commandments, " . . . the second is like unto it, Thou shalt love thy neighbour as thyself" (Matt. 22:39). If we really love our neighbor, we will want to share with him the message of salvation. I must add a personal note. The greatest good that has ever been done to me, or for me, in this world was done by the man who brought me the message of salvation, the message we call the gospel. He loved me; he was concerned for my good in this world and in the world to come. The Christ of this message changed my life, my home, and thank God, my destination.

In God-centered evangelism our motive is important. Evangelism is a good work; therefore, it must be done:

1. by a *right rule* — the Word of God.
2. with a *right end in view* — the glory of God.
3. with a *right motive* — love to God and love to man.

I am convinced that many of our churches would not be in the spiritual condition they are in if our past evangelism had been done by a God-centered rule, with a God-centered end in view, and by God-centered motives.

Evangelism is a good work and, like all our work, will be tried as to what sort it is. "Every man's work shall be made manifest: for the day shall declare it, because it shall be revealed by fire; and the fire shall try every man's work of what sort it is" (I Cor. 3:13).

2. THE GOAL OF EVANGELISM AS MANDATED BY OUR LORD

Then the eleven disciples went away into Galilee, into a mountain where Jesus had appointed them. And when they saw him, they worshipped him: but some doubted. And Jesus came and spake unto them, saying, All power is given unto me in heaven and in earth. Go ye therefore, and teach all nations, baptizing them in the name of the Father, and of the Son, and of the Holy Ghost: Teaching them to observe all things whatsoever I have commanded you: and lo, I am with you alway, even unto the end of the world. Amen.

— Matt. 28:16–20

I want to begin to examine what is commonly called the "Great Commission." We have this commission or mandate given in all four Gospels and the first chapter of Acts. Each place it is given in different words and gives us a different aspect of the clear command. We will begin by considering the goal of evangelism as found in Matthew 28:16–20.

In Matthew 28:17, we read, " . . . they worshipped him. . . ." Note: they worshipped before they witnessed. True evangelism is the overflow of a devotional life.

"And Jesus came up and spoke to them, saying, All authority has been given to Me in heaven and earth. Go therefore and make disciples, of all the nations, baptizing them in the name of the Father and the Son and the Holy Spirit,

5

teaching them to observe all that I commanded you: and low, I am with you always even to the end of the age" (vv. 18–20 NASB).

The goal of evangelism has three very clear, distinct parts, and it is not our prerogative to leave out any one of them.

MAKE DISCIPLES

The first part of the goal is to "Go and make disciples" or "Go and teach all nations," seeking to bring men into a *right relationship to the Son of God.* Let us be clear as to what constitutes a disciple. The usual definition says, "a disciple is a learner," but that is not an adequate definition. One may learn the teachings of Descartes and not be a disciple. One may intellectually learn the teachings of Jesus and not be His disciple. Therefore, let me give a full definition. A disciple, in the biblical sense, is:

1. A learner of the teachings.
2. A follower of the teacher.
3. One who is seeking to be conformed to the teacher and the teachings.

Being a disciple is more than giving a little nod to Jesus or learning a few religious shibboleths.

BAPTIZE THEM

The second part of the goal is just as clear as the first, ". . . baptizing them. . . ." And what is that? It is a church ordinance, and it is, among other things, *the badge of membership* into the Christian church. Even those who differ on the mode and the meaning of baptism agree on this point, that baptism is *the badge of membership* into the Christian church. Yes, it is a church ordinance. It was not given to the Boy Scouts, or the Y.M.C.A., or any of the so-called "para-church" organizations (*para* is a prefix meaning "beside" or "along side of"). These organizations (thousands of them) claim to be "right arms of the church."

Beyond dispute, the church is the God-appointed agent of evangelism, and part of the goal as we have it in Matthew 28:19-20 is to bring men into a *right relationship to the church of God.* It is not our prerogative to omit this part of the Great Commission. Any evangelistic organization or effort that ignores the second part of this commission in its goal cannot be considered to be biblical or God-centered. And, I am convinced that the blatant disregard by many of these so-called "para-church" organizations for this clear biblical truth is no small part of our problems in Christendom at this very hour. I stated before that this examination would show some shocking things, and I would plead the Scriptures as the court of appeal.

When Martin Luther left the Roman Catholic Church, he did not form "Luther Crusade for Christ, Inc." or some-other tax-free corporation for Christ. He (Christ) founded a church. When our missionaries go to the mission field they have this part of the goal as their goal.

When Peter, as spokesman of the Twelve, gave that great classic confession, ". . . Thou art the Christ, the Son of the living God," Jesus did not say, "Now you must form Simon Peter, Inc. for Christ," but rather, Jesus said, ". . . I will build my church . . . ," and the church of which He spoke was an organization. This is clear from the context, which tells us that Jesus went on to assign "the keys of the kingdom of Heaven" to the apostles (Matt. 16:16-19).

There was an organized church at Antioch, and Paul and Barnabas were sent out as missionaries, by both the Holy Spirit and the church: ". . . when they had fasted and prayed, and laid their hands on them, *they sent them away* . . ." (Acts 13:3).

Christ founded a church: ". . . I will build my *church* . . ." (Matt. 16:18). Christ loved the church and gave Himself for the church: " . . . Christ also loved the *church,* and gave himself for it" (Eph. 5:25). Christ is the head of the church:

7

"even as Christ is the *head* of the church . . ." (Eph. 5:23);
" . . . the *church* of the living God, the pillar and ground of the truth" (I Tim. 3:15).

Again, the church is the God-appointed agent of evangelism. I am well aware that the term "church" has at least two meanings, and although they are inseparable, they are properly distinguished from each other. Both the church as an organization operating through its special offices, and the church as an organism of believers, each of which holds a general or universal office, are God-ordained agents of evangelism. The New Testament makes that clear. In Asia Minor Paul and Barnabas ordained elders in every church (Acts 14:23). The Bible clearly teaches that evangelism is a task of the organized church.

There is not one "specialist" organization in the New Testament such as we have today. The church ministered to the whole family — men, women, young people, and children.

There were different gifts within the church, but they were not "para-church" organizations.

How do most of the so-called "para-church" organizations strengthen the church? They take away some of the best young people, the best men and women. They syphon off money, time, and talent and are not authorized to do so by Christ or the Scriptures. They weaken the church — many ignore this second part of our Lord's commission of seeking to bring men into a *right relationship to the church of God.*

I mentioned before that "para" is a prefix meaning "beside" or "along side of." Well, in medicine, it has another meaning. It means "a faulty or disordered condition; abnormal; as in paranoia" (Webster). I believe this medical definition will prove to be more accurate than the other for most "para-church" organizations. I am aware that God has used some of these organizations, but the best men in

8

the better "para-church" organizations recognize the church as the God-appointed agent of evangelism, and they do seek to point men and women to Bible preaching churches.

TEACH THEM

The third part of the Great Commission is ". . . teaching them to observe all that I command you. . . ." And what is this? Seeking to bring them into a *right relationship to the Word of God*.

"Teaching them . . ." is a life-long ministry. Jesus defines a disciple in these words: "Then said Jesus to those Jews which believed on him, If ye continue in my word, then are ye my disciples indeed; And ye shall know the truth and the truth shall make you free" (John 8:31, 32). There must be a continuing in the Word and growing in grace. This is why Christians need to be under sound preaching and teaching. This is the means to bring them into a *right relationship to the Word of God* and the God of the Word.

The *goal* of evangelism is very clear, and we can summarize it from the passage we are considering (Matt. 28:16–20):

1. Make disciples — seeking to bring them into a *right relationship to the Son of God*.
2. Baptize them (a church ordinance) — seeking to bring them into a *right relationship to the church of God*.
3. Teach them — seeking to bring them into a *right relationship to the Word of God*.

Anything less than this clearly defined *goal* is not biblical evangelism and, therefore, is not God-centered evangelism. All true, biblical, God-centered evangelism must have these three aspects as the *goal* of evangelism as clearly set forth by Christ in the text that we have considered.

3. THE SCOPE AND RESULTS OF EVANGELISM

And he said unto them, Go ye into all the world, and preach the gospel to every creature. He that believeth and is baptized shall be saved; but he that believeth not shall be damned.

— Mark 16:15, 16

In Matthew 28:16–20, Jesus gave us the *goal of evangelism*. In Mark 16:15, 16, we have the *scope* and *results*. The *scope* is very clear — *all the world* and *every creature*. The gospel is addressed to "whosoever will" (Rev. 22:17). There are two *results*: (1) " . . . he that believeth and is baptized shall be saved." (2) " . . . he that believeth not shall be damned." Salvation is one result, and damnation is another result.

Therefore, when the biblical gospel is preached, there will be *results,* and *God will be glorified.* His saving love and mercy will be glorified in the salvation of some; His justice, holiness, and righteousness will be glorified in the damnation of those who believe not. Many modern preachers do not like even to mention this aspect of the results, but it is clear in the Bible. When God reveals His mercy, He also always reveals His judgment, and the Bible makes this very clear. "Now thanks be unto God, which always causeth us to triumph in Christ, and maketh manifest the savour of his knowledge by us in every place. For we are unto God a sweet savour of Christ, in them that are saved, and in them that perish: To the one we are the savour of death unto death;

11

and to the other the savour of life unto life. And who is sufficient for these things?'' (II Cor. 2:14–16).

We have many examples of this same truth in the Bible. At the Red Sea — God's mercy was manifest in the salvation of some, and His justice was manifest in the damnation of others. At the time of the flood, His mercy was manifest in the salvation of Noah and his family, but His justice was manifest in the destruction of others. At Sodom, when in justice, He rained fire and brimstone, He also manifest His saving mercy to Lot.

The supreme example is the cross, where God's justice was manifest in His hatred for sin when He sheathed the sword of divine justice in the bosom of the Son of God. The very base of the cross is eternal justice; yet at the same place and at the same time, His saving love and mercy to poor sinners was manifest. The Spirit of the cross is eternal love. Both eternal justice and eternal love flow from the same cross.

Our Lord Himself took great comfort and consolation from the fact that God the Father would be glorified, even when He and His message were rejected. See this in Matthew 11:16–30. In verses 16 through 24, we see that our Lord and His message were rejected. What did Jesus do? According to Matthew 11:25–30, He did three things (now bear in mind, He and His message were rejected vv. 16–24):

First, He uttered a prayer of thanks (Matt. 11:25, 26); ''At that time Jesus answered and said, I thank thee, O Father, Lord of heaven and earth, because thou hast hid these things from the wise and prudent, and hast revealed them unto babes. Even so, Father: for so it seemed good in thy sight.'' (Luke's account says, ''He rejoiced in Spirit.'')

Second, He made a claim (Matt. 11:27): ''All things are delivered unto me of my Father: and no man knoweth the Son, but the Father; neither knoweth any man the Father, save the Son, and he to whomsoever the Son will reveal him.''

Third, he gave an invitation (Matt. 11:28-30): "Come unto me, all ye that labour and are heavy laden, and I will give you rest. Take my yoke upon you, and learn of me; for I am meek and lowly in heart: and ye shall find rest unto your souls. For my yoke is easy, and my burden is light.''

Mark gives us the *results* of the heavenly mandate — salvation or damnation. May God help us to be faithful to the command of Christ to take the message to all the world and take consolation in the fact that God will be glorified regardless of the results (II Cor. 2:14-16).

Yes, to some the gospel will be a savour of life unto life — *salvation*. To others it will be a savour of death unto death — *damnation*.

Be sure, if we obey this heavenly mandate, God will be glorified. When Moses prayed to see the glory of God (Exod. 33:17-19), God showed him these two things — *salvation* and *damnation*. "And he said, I will make all my goodness pass before thee, and I will proclaim the name of the LORD before thee; and will be gracious to whom I will be gracious, and will shew mercy on whom I will shew mercy" (Exod. 33:19). The apostle Paul gives us this same truth in Romans 9:15-18, when he quotes from the same account in Exodus.

Our Lord, in Mark, chapter 16, gives us the *scope* of biblical evangelism — *all the world* and *every creature*; and the *results* — *salvation* or *damnation*.

4. DOCTRINAL CONTENT OF THE MESSAGE OF EVANGELISM

And said unto them, Thus it is written, and thus it behoved Christ to suffer, and to rise from the dead the third day: And that repentance and remission of sins should be preached in his name among all nations, beginning at Jerusalem. And ye are witnesses of these things.

— Luke 24:46–48

Biblical doctrine is the foundation of evangelism as it is the foundation of Christian experience, Christian worship, Christian behavior, and Christian service.

There are three areas of biblical truth found in Luke 24:46–48, and what we believe about these three areas of truth will have a profound effect upon the *message* and the *methods* for evangelism.

We have considered the *goal* as we find it in Matthew 28:16–20, and the *scope* and *results* as we find them in Mark 16:15, 16. Now we will look at the *doctrinal content of the message* of evangelism as we consider the heavenly mandate in Luke 24:46–48.

In verse 48, Jesus said, "And ye are witnesses of these *things*." What *things* does He speak of? We must back up to answer that question. In verses 46 and 47, we learn what *things* we are witnesses of, and thus we have the *doctrinal content* of our Lord's mandate.

In verses 46 and 47, we have three basic areas of Christian truth that contain the vital and essential content of the

15

message of evangelism.

First, (v. 46) "it behoved Christ to suffer": *the cross*. The message includes all the truths that hinge on the suffering of Christ on the *cross*. What actually took place at the cross? —the atonement in its design, its accomplishments, and its application.

Second, (v. 46) "and to rise again from the dead": *the resurrection*. The message includes all the truths that hinge on the *resurrection* of our Lord. He ascended and is exalted to a throne — He is now the enthroned Christ. This will immediately bring us to proclaim His lordship. The resurrection establishes His lordship *now*.

Third, (v. 47) "And that repentance and remission of sins should be preached in His name among all nations": *repentance and remission*. Repentance — what is repentance? Whatever it is (we shall take it up later), it is part of the *message* of evangelism, and it involves the nature of saving faith.

It is the content of the message that needs to be carefully examined in our day. Therefore, I am going to spend more time on the *doctrinal content of the message* of evangelism. Let us take a serious look at these three areas of truth as we have them in Luke 24:46–48.

TRUTHS THAT HINGE ON THE DEATH OF CHRIST

The first area of truth is in verse 46: "it behoved Christ to suffer" — *the death of Christ on the cross, or the atonement.*

Demands of the Law

The law is the first message of the cross. There are three truths of the Bible that stand or fall together. They are *the law of God summarized in the Ten Commandments, the cross,* and *the righteous judgment of almighty God*. Why do I say that these three truths stand or fall together? Because you cannot touch one without touching the others.

1. If you do away with the Ten Commandments, there is no such thing as sin (". . . sin is the transgression of the Law" — I John 3:4). If there is no sin, the cross is not necessary.

2. If you do away with the cross, you have no answer to the sin question, and there is no hope for sinners.

3. If you do away with the righteous judgment of almighty God, who cares about *sin*, the *cross*, or *Christ?* The *law* is the first message of the cross.

Probably the verse in the Bible that best describes the work of Christ is Isaiah 42:21: ". . . he [Christ] will magnify the law and make it honorable." Christ magnified the law in His life by keeping it perfectly, and in His death by suffering its penalty for *His* people. The very base of the cross is Christ satisfying divine justice (the righteous demands of a Holy God) for sinners. At the cross, God the Father sheathed the sword of divine justice in the bosom of His Son in order that sinners might have an honorable pardon: not just sin overlooked, but sin paid for; not only expiation, but also propitiation.

This leads to a question in respect to the present-day evangelistic messages. Where is the preaching of the law? Paul said, ". . . by the law is the knowledge of sin" (Rom. 3:20). And in his testimony he acknowledged the law as the means that brought home the knowledge of sin. ". . . I had not known sin, but by the law . . ." (Rom. 7:7). *Where is the evangelistic preaching of the law?*

Luther said: "The Law must be laid upon those that are to be justified, that they may be shut up in the prison thereof, until the righteousness of faith come — that, when they are cast down and humbled by the Law, they should fly to Christ. The Lord humbles them, not to their destruction, but to their salvation. For God woundeth, that He may heal again. He killeth that He may quicken again."

Augustine said: "The conscience is not to be healed, if it be not wounded. Thou preachest and presseth the Law, the judgment to come, with much earnestness and importunity. He which hears, if he be not terrified, if he be not troubled, is not to be comforted."

Beza said: "Men are ever to be prepared for the gospel by the preaching of the Law."

John Calvin on the moral law:

> The true knowledge of God constrains us to worship Him, and that the true knowledge of self leads to genuine humility and self-abasement. The law is the instrument which the Lord uses to bring about both these results: by asserting therein His right to command, He calls us to pay Him the reverence due to His majesty; and by setting before us the standard of His righteousness, He shows us our unrighteousness and impotence. Moreover, the things which are taught in the tables of the law are also taught by that inward law which is written on the tables of every man's heart; for our conscience does not allow us to sleep an unbroken sleep, but inwardly testifies to us of the claims of God and of the difference between right and wrong. But since this inward law is insufficient, through our ignorance, pride, and self-love, God has given us also the plainer and surer testimony of the written law. From the law we learn that God, being our Creator, justly claims all that is due to a Father and a Master, namely, honor, reverence, love and fear: that we are not our own masters, at liberty to follow the desires of our own mind without regard to His good pleasure: finally, that He loveth righteousness and hateth iniquity, and that we therefore must follow after righteousness in the whole course of our life unless we would be guilty of impious ingratitude to our Maker. Nor can we rightly excuse ourselves by alleging our in-

ability to keep His law, seeing that the glory of God must not be measured by the extent of our powers, and that the sin which causes our inability lies within our own heart and is righteously imputed to us alone.

Therefore, we cannot exclude the first message of the cross, God's holy law, when we consider "these things which we are witnesses of."

We have considered just one aspect of the cross, that is, the base of the cross which is Christ satisfying the demands of the law, thus satisfying divine justice that sinners might have an honorable pardon: ". . . he shall magnify the Law and make it honorable" (Isa. 42:21).

Atonement

The next aspect of the cross that forms part of the doctrinal content of the divinely inspired message is the *atonement*. For whom did Christ die? The Bible is very clear on this answer, though many preachers are not.

The atonement that we are considering is a planned atonement — the cross was not an accident. God planned it. He was not sleeping or caught off guard at the cross. He had an unchangeable, immutable plan, and it was being carried out. The apostle Peter preached this as part of his first message: "Him, being delivered by the determinate counsel and foreknowledge of God, ye have taken, and by wicked hands have crucified and slain" (Acts 2:23).

The apostles not only preached it; they prayed it. Hear their prayer in Acts 4:27–29: "For of a truth against thy holy child Jesus, whom thou hast anointed, both Herod, and Pontius Pilate, with the Gentiles, and the people of Israel, were gathered together, *for to do whatsoever thy hand and thy counsel determined before to be done.*" God was the master of ceremonies at the cross.

Jesus also taught that God the Father had an unchangeable, immutable plan:

> For I came down from heaven, not to do mine own will, but the will of Him that sent me. And this is the Father's will which hath sent me, that *of all which he hath given me,* I should lose nothing, but should raise it up again at the last day (John 6:38, 39).

> I am the good shepherd: the good shepherd giveth his life for the *sheep* (John 10:11).

> I know my *sheep* (John 10:14-15).

Jesus makes clear why some do not believe on Him. Have you ever wondered why some do not believe? Well, Jesus answers that question here:

> But ye believe not, because ye are not of my *sheep*, as I said unto you (John 10:26).

He describes two characteristics of His *sheep:*

> My sheep *hear* my voice [a disposition to know His will], and they *follow* me [a disposition to do His will] (John 10:27).

This truth, that the atonement was for the *sheep*, is underscored by our Lord's prayer found in John 17. Hear His prayer: "As thou hast given him power over all flesh, that he should give eternal life *to as many as thou hast given him*" (John 17:2). "I pray for them: I pray not for the world, but *for them which thou hast given me:* for they are thine" (John 17:9). "Father, I will that they also, *whom thou hast given me,* be with me where I am; that they may behold my glory, which thou hast *given* me: for thou lovedst me before the foundation of the world" (John 17:24).

This view of the extent of the atonement makes the cross a place of victory, because what the Father planned, the Son purchased, and these He prays for. This is consistent with that great declaration in that messianic prophesy of His coming: "He shall see of the travail of his soul, and shall be satisfied: by his knowledge shall my righteous servant just- ify many; for he shall bear their iniquities" (Isa. 53:11).

Jesus teaches the same thing in John 6:37: "All that the Father *giveth* me *shall come* to me. . . ." Not, maybe they will come, or, it would be nice if they came, or, if they decide they will come, but rather, *"shall come."* This, then, is an important element of the message of the cross, the message of evangelism. This means that Christ's death was not in vain, but rather, everyone for whom He savingly died, *will come.* It is interesting to note that when the angel an- nounced His birth to Joseph, the angel was straight on this point: "And she shall bring forth a son, and thou shalt call his name *Jesus:* for he shall *save his people* from their sins" (Matt. 1:21).

Please note the text says, *"save his people,"* not every single individual, but *His people—the sheep.*

God used the fact that He had some people, some sheep, to encourage the evangelizing of that wicked city of Cor- inth. The great apostle was afraid to go to Corinth, and God encouraged him by saying, ". . . be not afraid . . . for I am with thee, and no man shall set on thee to hurt thee: for I have much *people* in this city" (Acts 18:9, 10).

1. His coming was *for His people* (Matt. 1:21): "And she shall bring forth a son, and thou shalt call his name Jesus: for he shall save his people from their sins."

2. His purchase on the Cross was for the *sheep* — His people (John 10:11, 14, 15): "I am the good shepherd: the good shepherd giveth his life for the sheep. . . . I am the good shepherd, and know my sheep, and am known of mine. As the Father knoweth me, even so know I the Father: and I lay down my life for the sheep."

3. His prayer was for *all that the Father gave Him* (John 17:2, 9): "As thou hast given him power over all flesh, that he should give eternal life to as many as thou hast given him . . . I pray for them: I pray not for the world, but for them

which thou hast given me; for they are thine.''

Is this the message of the cross that you have heard — Christ whose death is not in vain and will not fail to accomplish all that was intended? Or, have you heard the message of a poor, impotent, pathetic, and sometimes, effeminate Jesus who died just to make salvation possible and who is standing idly and impotently by, waiting to see what these mighty, powerful sinners are going to do with Him?

This is not just a different emphasis. It is a different content of the message of evangelism. The biblical gospel is God-centered, God-honoring, and it will bring glory to God and good to sinners.

TRUTHS THAT HINGE ON THE RESURRECTION OF CHRIST

This brings us to the second doctrine in Luke 24:46–48: ''. . . and to rise again from the dead . . .'' — *the doctrine of the resurrection*. This sets forth Christ's exaltation and lordship, and all I will do at this point is show how the apostles had this key truth as part of the doctrinal content of their evangelistic message.

The first post-resurrection sermon is recorded in Acts 2. Peter is the preacher. He begins the sermon in verse 14: ''But Peter, standing up with the eleven, lifted up his voice, and said unto them. . . .'' Let us follow his sermon to underscore how faithful he was to our Lord's mandate in respect to the doctrinal content as we find it in Luke 24. Peter brings in the cross and the crucifixion: ''Him, being delivered by the determinate counsel and foreknowledge of God, ye have taken, and by wicked hands have crucified and slain.'' He emphasizes the resurrection: ''Whom God hath raised up having loosed the pains of death. . . . This Jesus hath God raised up, whereof we all are witnesses.'' He also emphasizes the implications of the resurrection, that is, Christ's exaltation to a throne and His lordship: ''. . . He would raise up Christ to sit on his throne. . . . being by the right hand of God exalted. . . . Therefore let all the house of Israel know assuredly, that God hath made that same Jesus, whom ye have crucified, both Lord and Christ." You will note that Peter preached that Christ is presently Lord, and not by man's making or consent, but by almighty God's decree: "God hath made that same Jesus, whom ye have crucified, both Lord and Christ." Please note carefully that *men* do not make Christ Lord. God almighty has already done it. Therefore, Christ must be preached as *Lord* at the outset in the evangelistic message.

Now, it is just at this point that we will see how different the present message of evangelism really is. Lordship was in the initial message—at the outset—not some second act of consecration. There was bowing at the beginning. This is very clearly seen in Luke, where our Lord gives the doctrinal content for the message of God-centered evangelism (Luke 24:46, 47). God-centered evangelism must have the God-given doctrinal content in the message.

The lordship of Christ is a vital part of the message of evangelism. There are those who call this the "lordship gospel," and those who preach the lordship of Christ "lordship preachers." I would to God there were no other kind! Our churches would not be filled with so many who give no biblical evidence of conversion. No one will be saved who has not bowed to the lordship of Christ, any more than one could be saved without repentance. "I tell you, Nay: but, except ye repent, ye shall all likewise perish" (Luke 13:3).

I will appeal to the sacred manual of evangelism, that is, the Book of Acts, to support this truth. In Acts, chapter one, our Lord goes back to heaven (Acts 1:10). Immediately, the apostles became authorized custodians of our Lord's message and His mission. This is at the very pure source of the stream before the present, man-made corruptions clouded the message and contaminated the pure stream of biblical evangelism.

It seems that every Bible-believing person would agree that if we want to examine the message of evangelism, we should study and consider what the apostles preached; therefore, my appeal will be to the Book of Acts. I will direct your attention to three salient points concerning the lordship of Christ.

First, when our Lord was introduced and announced into the world as to who He is, it was a clear announcement of His *lordship:*

> For unto you is born this day in the city of David a Savior, which is Christ the *Lord* (Luke 2:11).

That Savior is the Lord, and the Lord is the Savior. And saviorhood and lordship are inseparably joined. There is only one mediator, and Christ is that mediator. As our mediator, He has three offices: Prophet, Priest and King. But we are not saved by one of His offices — we are saved by *Him.* "He that hath the Son hath life," not, "He that hath one of His offices hath life." If we are in Him, we have the blessing and benefit of all His offices.

Second, when the New Testament preachers preached, they preached the lordship of Christ:

> For we preach not ourselves but Christ Jesus the Lord . . . (II Cor. 4:5).

And there is not one place in the whole New Testament where Christ is offered as we hear Him offered today —"trust Christ as your personal Savior." There is no such language used by the apostles; not even is there such an idea conveyed.

Third, when believers came to Christ in the New Testament, they came to Him as Lord:

> As you have therefore received Christ Jesus the Lord, so walk ye in Him (Col. 2:6).

Lordship was not a second step of consecration, or a second work of grace. Nor did sinners make Him *Lord*. He is Lord by God almighty's decree, irrespective of anything sinners did, said, or believed. Acts 2:36 should settle this question as to who makes Jesus *Lord:* "Therefore let all the house of Israel know assuredly, that *God hath made that same Jesus, whom ye have crucified, both Lord and Christ."*

Again, I would like to appeal to the Book of Acts where we have the purest examples of evangelism, as to message, methods and motives. It will shock some of today's evangelists and their man-invented, unbiblical, Hollywood methods to find that the word "Savior" appears only two times in the Acts of the Apostles, and in neither case (Acts 5:31; 13:23) is it connected with sinners "accepting Jesus as your personal Savior."

How in God's name did we come to huckstering off Jesus as some kind of hell-insurance policy, when the Bible announced Him as *Lord* and exalted Him to a throne? The New Testament preachers preached His *lordship,* and sinners received him as *Lord*. There is not one New Testament example of Christ being offered any other way. This is a vital point, and not just some "preachers' hobby." Oh! the *lordship* of *Christ* is the lost doctrine of the Bible in evangelism.

One of the greatest soul winners that ever lived, Charles Haddon Spurgeon, warned young preachers in his school about this perversion that we see in much evangelism today. He said,

> If the professed convert distinctly and deliberately declares that he knows the Lord's will, but does not mean to attend to it, you are not to pamper his presumptions, but it is your duty to assure him that he is not saved. Do not suppose that the Gospel is magnified or God-glorified by going to the worldlings and telling them that they may be saved at this mo-

25

ment by simply "accepting Christ" as their Savior, while they are wedded to their idols, and their hearts are still in love with sin. If I do so, I tell them a lie, pervert the Gospel, insult Christ, and turn the grace of God into lasciviousness. It is interesting to notice that the Apostles preached the Lordship of Christ. The word "Savior" occurs only twice in the Acts of the Apostles (Acts 5:31, 13:23). On the other hand it is amazing to notice the title "Lord" is mentioned 92 times; "Lord Jesus" 13 times; and "The Lord Jesus Christ" 6 times in the same book. The Gospel is: "Believe on the Lord Jesus Christ, and thou shalt be saved."

The following New Testament statistics should settle the question. Jesus is referred to as Lord 822 times; Lord Jesus, 22 times; and Lord Jesus Christ, 81 times.

The word *Savior* is only used 24 times (8 of which refer to God the Father as our Savior).

Matthew Henry, that memorable household commentator, said in the introduction to his commentary on the New Testament, "All the grace contained in this book [New Testament] is owning to Jesus Christ as our Lord and Savior; and, unless we consent to Him as our Lord, we cannot expect any benefit by Him as our Saviour."

Yes, He is Savior, and our personal Savior, but His saviorhood is within His lordship and not apart from it. This is one of the weak links in the present-day message of evangelism. Yet, it is the principal doctrine that hinges on the resurrection—Jesus' exaltation, His lordship.

If you don't agree with this point now, you will! "Wherefore God also hath highly exalted Him, and given Him a name which is above every name: That at the name of Jesus, every knee should bow, of things in heaven, and things in earth, and things under the earth; and that every tongue should confess that Jesus Christ is Lord, to the glory of God the Father" (Phil. 2:9–11). Some will acknowledge His lordship in *restitution* now, but *all* will acknowledge it in *recognition* later.

God-centered evangelism proclaims the biblical message of the *lordship of Christ* at the outset, not as a second work of grace, or an act of optional consecration later.

REPENTANCE AND REMISSION

Let us now consider the third element of the doctrinal content as we have it in Luke 24:47: "And that *repentance* and remission of sins should be preached in His name among all nations, beginning at Jerusalem."

Repentance is one of the vital elements of the gospel message that is strangely absent from most of the present-day evangelism, both personal evangelism and mass or public evangelism. This essential ingredient of gospel preaching has slowly, but surely, faded from our present-day pulpits. As a result of this missing element, our church rolls are filled with many members who have missed *repentance* and will perish unless they repent. Jesus said to the religious crowd of His day, "I tell you, no, but, unless you *repent*, you will all likewise perish" (Luke 13:3, NASB). This is just as true today as when Jesus said it.

Consider the place *repentance* had in New Testament preaching.

Our Lord's Example

Repentance was our Lord's first and last subject. Early in His ministry He called for repentance:

> From that time Jesus began to preach, and to say, Repent: for the kingdom of heaven is at hand (Matt. 4:17).

> . . . Jesus came into Galilee, preaching the gospel of the kingdom of God, and saying, The time is fulfilled, and the kingdom of God is at hand: repent ye, and

believe the gospel (Mark 1:14, 15).

His last instruction to His successors was for them to preach repentance:

> And that repentance and remission of sins should be preached in his name among all nations, beginning at Jerusalem (Luke 24:47).

Does this fact not show how important repentance is? How can a minister claim to be preaching the gospel if he leaves out one-half the ingredients? Our Lord made it His keynote address (Matt. 4:17; Mark 1:15), and His disciples followed His example and His clear instructions.

The Apostolic Example

The apostles took seriously our Lord's instructions. We see it from the very first sermon after His ascension (Acts 2:14–41). The apostle Peter was the preacher. The Holy Spirit had come in convicting power; the audience was smitten in conscience (Acts 2:27) and inquired what they must do to be saved. Now, most evangelists in our day would have said, "Accept Jesus as your personal Savior," a form of words not found once in the New Testament and which excludes this imperative to repent. Peter was more interested in obeying the Lord's instruction than in results or statistics. Therefore, Peter answered their question by saying, "repent." He was taught biblical evangelism by our Lord as we can clearly learn from Mark 6:12, "And they went out, and preached that men should repent."

The apostles never changed their message regardless of their audience. To the intellectual Stoics and Epicureans at Athens, the great apostle Paul said, "God . . . now commandeth *all* men [Jew or Gentile] everywhere to repent." This was not optional, but essential. Jesus taught the apostles, "Except you *repent* you will *perish*" (Luke 13:3). He taught men to preach *repentance*. He set the example by preaching *repentance* Himself. How have we lost the message of repentance in our evangelism?

In Peter's second sermon (Acts 3) we see he had not forgotten or changed the message. See it in Acts 3:19. "Repent ye therefore, and be converted, that your sins may be blotted out. . . ." Again, it is clear that repentance is part of true conversion and connected with forgiveness of sins. May I encourage every serious person to turn to the Book of Acts to confirm what I am saying. Surely, no one would disagree with me when I say the Book of Acts in the inspired manual for God-centered evangelism.

Let me give you another example from the sacred manual of evangelism — Acts 20:20, 21. The context of these verses describes our Lord's chief apostle leaving the church at Ephesus where he had evangelized for three years, and he is recounting his ministry and message to the elders as part of his parting words. He gives them the content of his evangelistic message in these words, ". . . have taught you publicly, and from house to house, testifying both to the Jews, and also to the Greeks [Gentiles], repentance toward God and faith toward our Lord Jesus Christ."

This passage alone should forever establish the fact that repentance is:

1. An inseparable part of the message of evangelism.
2. Not just for the Jew but also for the Gentile.
3. A sacred duty.
4. Inseparable from faith.

Another apostolic example in the life of the great apostle is Acts 26:18-20. The apostle is giving his personal testimony before King Agrippa, and he tells the king what Jesus told him to do, that is, the purpose for which our Lord had appeared to him; Jesus said, ". . . I have appeared unto thee for this purpose, to make thee a minister and a witness . . ." (v. 16). In verses 18-20, our Lord tells Paul what his ministry was meant to be: "To open their eyes, and to turn them from darkness to light, and from the power of Satan unto God, that they may receive forgiveness of sins. . ." (v. 18). In verse 20, Paul tells King Agrippa the content of the message, ". . .that they should *repent* and turn to God . . .", not just trust, but *turn* and trust.

Now, this message of repentance almost got Paul killed. "For these causes the Jews caught me in the temple, and went about to kill me" (v. 21). And one of the reasons preachers avoid preaching repentance is this very point. It will cause some waves and some antagonism from this generation of poor, lost, self-deceived church members who are products of an evangelism that has left repentance out of its message. Therefore, the supposed converts have missed Bible repentance, and their life and their dedication to Christ and His church testify that they do not perform deeds appropriate to repentance.

I am making a plea for every sincere Christian to examine all personal evangelism and public evangelistic preaching by this clear, New Testament, God-centered evangelistic message. Many of our serious church leaders and members know that there is something wrong with most of the so-called "converts," but they do not seem to trace the problem to the message of evangelism. This is why they are forever rushing on the contemporary scene with some new method while the real problem is in the message.

The harvest of poor, lost church members that we have reaped is a result of the seeds that have been sown — seeds that did not include what our Lord clearly commanded to be part of the Great Commission (Luke 24:46, 47). Our Christian forefathers would unequivocally agree with the truth of what I am seeking to set forth. The following is a quote from an old Southern Baptist Declaration of Faith:

> We believe that Repentance and Faith are sacred duties, and also inseparable graces, wrought in our souls by the regenerating Spirit of God; whereby being

deeply convicted of our (1) guilt, (2) danger, and (3) helplessness, and of (4) the Way of Salvation by Christ, we turn to God with unfeigned (1) contrition, (2) confession; and supplication for Mercy; at the same time heartily receiving the Lord Jesus Christ as our Prophet, Priest, and King, and relying on Him alone as the only, and all sufficient Savior.

This is a far cry from that anemic, unbiblical expression, "accept Jesus as your personal Savior."

Since repentance is one of the missing links in much modern evangelism, and some teachers and preachers pervert the meaning, I want to present what the president of the first Southern Baptist Seminary, Dr. James P. Boyce, taught about it. But, first, let me underscore my premise that not only is it a missing link, but the message which replaces it is badly perverted. The following quote will prove it.

Any teaching that demands a change of conduct toward either God or man for salvation is to add works or human effort to faith, and this contradicts all Scripture and is an accursed message.

The above quote is from a book entitled *Handbook of Personal Evangelism* by Dr. A. Ray Stanford (onetime president of Florida Bible College), Dr. Richard A. Seymour (President, Soul Winning Seminars) and Miss Carol Ann Streib. The book was the textbook on evangelism for the Florida Bible College, and it is a fair representation of much shallow, man-centered evangelism.

You will note Dr. Boyce says that the doctrine of repentance must be learned two ways. First from the Greek word itself, and second, from its application to a matter which is written within the sphere of morals. The following is from a chapter of *Abstract of Systematic Theology* by Dr. James

31

P. Boyce.[1]

The Scripture doctrine of repentance is to be learned in part from the meaning of the original Greek word used to express it, and in part from its application to a matter which is within the sphere of morals.

I. There are two forms of words used in the New Testament which are translated repent and repentance. Only one of these is used of the repentance associated with salvation from sin. This is the verb μετανοέω (metanoeo), and the corresponding noun μετάνοια (metanoia). The other verb is μεταμέλομαι (metamelomai), the noun of which does not appear in the New Testament, but occurs in the Septuagint in Hosea 11:8. The verb is used in the Septuagint in Psa. 110:4; and Jer. 20:16. It is also the word used in the New Testament in Matt. 21:29, which says of the son who had refused to obey his father's command to work in the vineyard, "afterward he repented himself and went." It likewise is found in Matt. 21:32 and 27:3, this latter being the case of Judas. Paul uses it in Rom. 11:29; and II Cor. 7:8–10. It is also the word used in Heb. 7:21. In all other places translated repent and repentance in the New Testament, the original is metanoeo or metanoia. This word means to reconsider to perceive afterwards, and hence to change one's view, and mind, or purpose, or even judgment, implying disapproval and abandonment of past opinions and purposes, and the adoption of others which are different. In all cases of inward change, there is not necessarily a change of outward conduct, nor is such change accompanied by

---

[1] *Abstract of Systematic Theology,* Dr. James P. Boyce Chap. XXXIII, "Repentance."

regret. These results of the inward change would flow from the nature of that about which that change has arisen.

We arrive therefore, at the meaning of Christian repentance partly through the meaning of these Greek words, but also partly because it is exercised about a question of morals. It is seen that it involves a change in the outward life because such change is a result of the change of inward opinions. It also includes sorrow for sin because a change of view as to the nature of sin and of holiness must be accompanied by regret and sorrow as to the past acts of sin.

The word μεταμέλομαι (metamelomai) means to change one's care, to regret; the idea of sorrow always accompanying it.

The two words are nearly synonymous in their secondary meaning, and each is used in this secondary meaning in the New Testament. Μετανοέω (metanoeo), however, traces the feeling of sorrow and the change of life back to an inward change of opinion and judgment as to the nature of sin and holiness, and of the relations of man and God. It is perhaps on this account that it is exclusively used for true repentance in the New Testament. This is not simply sorrow, or remorse, which may pass away, or lead in despair to other sins, or fill the soul with anxiety; but a heartfelt change in the inward soul towards God and holiness, which is lasting and effective, and which may be associated with peace and joy in believing.

II. To set forth more explicitly what Christian Repentance is, it may be stated that it includes:

1. An intellectual and spiritual perception of the opposition between holiness in God and sin in man. It does not look at sin as the cause of punishment, but, abhors it, because it is vile in the sight of God and involves in heinous guilt all who are sinners.

2. It consequently includes sorrow and self-loathing, and earnest desire to escape the evil of sin. The penitent soul does not so much feel the greatness of its danger as the greatness of it sinfulness.

3. It also includes an earnest turning to God for help and deliverance from sin, seeking pardon for guilt and aid to escape its presence.

4. It is also accompanied by deep regret because of the sins committed in the past, and by determination with God's help to avoid sin and live in holiness hereafter. The heart heretofore against God and for sin is now against sin and for God.

From these facts, it will be seen that:

(1) The seat of true repentance is in the soul. It is not of itself the mere intellectual knowledge of sin, nor the sorrow that accompanies it, nor the changed life that flows from it; but it is the soul's apprehension of its heinous character, which begets the horror and self-loathing which accompany it, and the determination to forsake sin which flows from it.

(2) That true repentance is inconsistent with the continuance in sin because of abounding grace.

(3) That true repentance consists of mental and spiritual emotion, and not of outward self-imposed chastisements. Even the pious life and devotion to God which follow are described not as repentance, but as fruits meet for repentance.

III. The Scriptures teach that the author of true repentance is God operating by truth upon the renewed heart.

Acts 5:31 — Christ is said to have been exalted "to give repentance to Israel, and remission of sins."

Acts 11:18 — "Then to the Gentiles also hath God granted repentance unto life."

The means used is the preaching and other exhibition of the truth. Repentance like faith comes through the hearing of the Word. By this men are exhorted to that duty, and gain the knowledge of the truths taught by God, through spiritual apprehension of which men are led to the truth.

Why do some verses just say *repent* (Mark 6:12; Acts 2:38; 3:19), others say *believe* and nothing about repentance (John 3;16, 18; Acts 8:37; 16:31;), and still others say *repent* and *believe* (Mark 1:15; Acts 20:21)?

The best way to answer this question is by quoting an Article of Faith from the Baptist Confession of 1833, called "The New Hampshire Confession." The following article was added to this confession in 1853:

Article VIII: Of Repentance and Faith

We believe that Repentance and Faith are sacred duties, and also *inseparable* graces, wrought in our souls by the regenerating Spirit of God; whereby, being deeply convinced of our guilt, danger and helplessness, and of the way of salvation by Christ, we turn to God with unfeigned contrition, confession and supplication for mercy; at the same time heartily receiving the Lord Jesus Christ as our Prophet, Priest and King, and relying on Him alone as the only and all sufficient Savior.

You will note that *repentance* and faith are *inseparable*

graces. Herein lies the answer to our question. This is just saying that the nature of saving faith includes *repentance.* Therefore, where there is no repentance, there is no saving faith. It is here that many, many poor lost church members are self-deceived. They have missed repentance and are as lost as lost can be. Many do not even know what repentance is; therefore, how could they possibly know if they have repented?

Let me further emphasize this "inseparableness" of faith and repentance from an old catechism question (Westminster Shorter Catechism):

Question 87.
What is repentance unto life?

Answer.
Repentance unto life is a saving grace, whereby a sinner, out of a true sense of his sin, and apprehension of the mercy of God in Christ, doth, with grief and hatred of his sin, turn from it unto God, with full purpose of and endeavor after, new obedience.

You will notice the phrase ". . . and the apprehension of the mercy of God in Christ. . . ." One might think it strange to find the necessity of grasping "the mercy of God in Christ" in a definition of repentance. Ah, but it only underscores the point that where "saving faith" is found, there evangelical repentance will be found also, and where evangelical repentance is found, there true saving faith will be found. They are Siamese twins—inseparable.

The word "repent" does not need to appear for us to see the principle of repentance as part of the message of God-centered evangelism. Let me illustrate it from our Lord's evangelism. In His personal evangelism to the rich young ruler (Mark 10:17–22), the rich young ruler wanted to know what to do to have eternal life (Mark 10:17). The *Master Evangelist* addresses Himself to the rich young ruler's question, but He did not use the words *believe* or *repent*. However He got to the heart of true repentance and saving faith by showing the rich young ruler that he could not have two Gods, and therefore, he must turn from his "green god." "Then Jesus beholding him loved him, and said unto him, one thing thou lackest: go thy way, sell whatsoever thou hast, and give to the poor, and thou shalt have treasure in heaven: and come, take up the cross, and follow me." This is preaching repentance, and it was necessary for the young man to turn *from* — as well as *to* — in order to have eternal life. Men must *repent* or *perish*!

Charles Haddon Spurgeon had a great sermon entitled "Turn or Burn" from the text Psalm 7:12: "If he turn not, he will whet his sword; he hath bent his bow, and made it ready." His outline for the sermon was:

1. The nature of the turning here meant.
2. The necessity there is for men's turning, otherwise God will punish them.
3. The means whereby men can be turned from the error of their ways.

Sometime ago, I read of a godly old minister who was nicknamed by his colleagues "Mr. Faith and Repentance." The reason for this nickname was that he dwelt much on these two inseparable graces. He used to say, "If I die in the pulpit, I hope I am preaching *faith* and *repentance*, and if I die out of the pulpit, I hope I die practicing *faith* and *repentance*.

Repentance is a missing link in much present-day evangelism; yet it is part of the doctrinal content of our message. It is not new methods that we need. It is the very message of evangelism that needs to be restored; not just a "tune-up," but a complete "overhaul."

Conversion must reach the *whole man*, and therefore, faith and repentance must also reach the *whole man*.

1. His *mind* — that is, what he thinks.
2. His *affections* — that is, what he feels.
3. His *will* — that is, what he decides.

5. THE AUTHORITY AND POWER FOR OUR COMMISSION TO EVANGELIZE

Then said Jesus to them again, Peace be unto you:
as my Father hath sent me, even so send I you.
And when he had said this, he breathed on them,
and saith unto them, Receive ye the Holy Ghost.
— John 20:21, 22

We come now to John where we have the *authority* and *power* for our commission.

In the context of John 20:21, 22, we have an account of our Lord's first appearance to the disciples after He rose from the dead. He had sent the news of His resurrection by trusted and credible messengers. But now He comes to them in person showing them His love and confirming their faith.

The first imperative for evangelism is *peace* in our own soul. He said, "*Peace* be unto you." He showed them the marks of the cross — the marks of sacrificial love. They were convinced and confirmed by His appearance: "We have seen the Lord." It made them glad: "Then were the disciples glad."

Verse 21 reads, ". . . as my Father hath sent me, even so send I you." Here is our authority: *"I send you."*

But, we need more than authority; we need *Power* to evangelize, and in verse 22, we see this also: "he *breathed* on them." This was sovereign, empowering *breath*. Only this breath can empower us and give life to dead sinners. It is that same breath that in the beginning (Gen. 2:7) made the difference between a lump of clay and a living soul. It is only this heavenly breath that can give life to poor, dead sinners, and recognizing this imperative will kill all carnal methods so common in man-centered evangelism.

The heavenly breath is necessary for life and labors. In the Old Testament, the Spirit is often compared to breath. Ezekiel was commanded to preach to dead bones. He prayed for the same breath, ". . . Come, O breath, and breathe upon these slain *that they may live*" (Ezek. 37:9).

Only if this breath comes can those who are dead in trespasses and sin live. Jesus showed them His hands and His side, but the plainest evidence will not convince anyone without the work of the heavenly Dove. Nor will the clearest evidence give power for the work of evangelism. The soldiers at the tomb were eye witnesses of the resurrection, but this did not convince or convert them. There was no converting power in the evidence.

Oh, for that heavenly breath! Oh, for Jesus to breathe on us for the work of evangelism, and breathe on those who are dead in trespasses and sin! "A man can receive nothing, except it be given him from heaven" (John 3:27). Humbling, very humbling both to the preacher and the hearer. But, it is also hopeful, very hopeful to the preacher and the hearer. There is something to be had. There is something from above, and it is not at the end of an accepted proposition, but in the hands of a living Christ.

> As thou has given him *power* over all flesh, that he should give eternal life to as many as thou hast given him (John 17:2).

Eternal life is in the hands of a living Christ. That should make sinners become beggars: "Lord, if thou wilt thou canst make me clean" (Luke 5:12); "God be merciful to me a sinner" (Luke 18:13).

Oh, for that quickening Spirit, that life-giving Spirit, that sanctifying Spirit to come upon us! Oh, for Jesus to breathe upon us afresh! This would change the screeching, impotent machinery of evangelism into saving power. This need should drive us to prayer.

In Luke 11, we have some instructions on prayer for the Spirit, and we have in those instructions a promise. "If ye then, being evil, know how to give good gifts unto your children: how much more shall your heavenly Father give the Holy Spirit to them that ask Him?" (Luke 11:13).

There is some relationship between prayer and that holy breath that we need in evangelism. If that heavenly wind blows, we will be able to say what the early Christians said in Acts 5:29–32, "And we are his witnesses of these things; and so is also the Holy Ghost, whom God hath given to them that obey him." There is some relationship between prayer and the Holy Spirit, and also some relationship between obedience and the Holy Spirit.

"As my Father hath sent me, even so send I you." Yes, there is some difference between our Lord's mission and ours. He came to offer Himself a sacrifice for sin, and by His blood to obtain eternal salvation for His sheep. There is always a way to cop out and hide when we use Christ or the apostles as examples by pointing out the difference. In many respects they were unique. We do not have the extraordinary gifts of the apostles or apostolic discernment.

However, though there are some unique differences, there are also many similarities. We have the same object, that is the glory of God and the good of man, and the same principle of obedience; and, above all, we need the same holy breath.

Jesus Himself could not do His work without the Holy Spirit. His preaching did not affect anything without the Holy Spirit.

The Spirit's process in translating a lost soul from the kingdom of darkness into the kingdom of God's dear Son consists of three steps or stages. These steps are not always discernable in time or in our experience, but we can set them

41

out separately from the Scriptures for study and for our understanding. They are:

1. Convincing the conscience of sin and misery.
2. Enlightening the mind.
3. Renewing the will.

No one is truly converted if he has not been convinced of sin; if his mind has not been enlightened, and his will not changed. Would not this exclude many of those poor, lost church members who have been numbered as converts? Anything less than this is not Bible conversion and leaves poor, benighted souls lost, deceived, doomed and damned. These three things may greatly differ as to:

1. Extent of conviction and enlightening—some may know very little, yet be truly converted and often greater conviction comes after conversion.
2. Duration — there is not a given length of time as to conviction, or a given number of days or weeks for enlightening of the mind.
3. Results — all true conversions do not produce the same fruit as to the usefulness or the amount of zeal.

This is all consistent with what the Scripture teaches us concerning the Spirit's mission to the world and to the church. Notice, I said "the *world* and the *church*." We must not be guilty of not recognizing the Spirit's ministry to both. This is clearly seen from our Lord's parting counsel to His own (John 16:6–14). After He tells them not to be sorrowful because He is going away, He tells them why: " . . .it is expedient for you that I go away. . . ." Then He tells them why it is expedient: " . . . for if I go not away, the Comforter will not come unto you."

He then very clearly tells them what the Holy Spirit would do when He would come in power, in respect to the *world*, note well, the *world*. He then gives us the mission of the Spirit to the *world*. He will " . . .convict the *world* in respect of sin, and of righteousness, and of judgment" (ASV).

Only the Spirit can do that which is essential to conversion. However, conviction alone is not conversion. Sometimes conviction is unto conversion, and sometimes, it is conviction unto condemnation. *Felix* was so much convicted that he trembled (Acts 24:25), but we have no record of his conversion. *Pilate* was so convicted that he tried to wash the innocent blood of Christ from his hands, but he was not converted. *King Agrippa* was convicted — ". . . almost thou persuadest me to be a Christian" — but we do not find that he was ever converted.

Here we see the mission of the Spirit to the world. Conviction is not conversion. One of the errors and weaknesses of man-centered evangelism is the lack of understanding on this point — the absolute necessity of the work of the Spirit, not only to convict, but to convince and convert.

Every true minister and church leader should be pained and concerned for those poor, benighted church members who are thought of by themselves, and pronounced by their teachers, to be Christians and yet know absolutely nothing about conviction of sin, righteousness and judgment to come. May God have mercy on these statistic-hungry preachers who are more interested in the statistical results that accrue to them than in the true biblical results of Holy Spirit conversion.

Thank God for those in the church who, though once unbelievers, deaf, blind and dead, are no longer aliens and strangers, but are fellow citizens of God. They know experimentally this converting work of the Spirit. They know the difference between themselves and the world. Their eyes have been opened and turned from darkness to light, from the power of Satan unto God.

They were reproved as one of the world, but now they have been guided and taught of Christ and His truth. Yes, they have passed through the Spirit's process of translating

43

a lost soul from the kingdom of darkness into the kingdom of God's dear Son. Their minds have been enlightened, their consciences have been convicted in respect to Christ and their sin, and their hearts and wills have been renewed.

This is God-centered evangelism — *knowing, preaching* and *practicing* the truth about the work of the Spirit in conversion.

Have you ever been truly evangelized?

Has your mind been enlightened in the knowledge of Christ?

Has your conscience been convicted of sin and its consequences?

Has your will been renewed by the power of the Spirit?

EFFECTUAL CALL

Our fathers called the work of the Spirit in bringing men to Christ the *effectual call* meaning that the call effected what it is intended to do. Only the Spirit can give this inward, or effectual call. When we evangelize by dispensing the Word, which is usually the outward means, we do not know who are included in the *election of grace,* that is, who the Spirit will effectually call. We give the gospel call, or invitation, to all men, indiscriminately. We draw the bow at a venture, but the Lord, who *"knoweth them that are His"* directs the arrow, so as to cause it to strike home to the hearts of those whom He *"hath chosen in Christ before the foundation of the world."*

This inward call of the Spirit is under the direction of the sovereign will and pleasure of God as to the *time* of it. Some are effectually called at the third hour; some at the sixth; some are called at the ninth; and some at the eleventh hour. Some, like good old Obadiah, have feared the Lord from their youth. Others, like Saul of Tarsus, have been born, as it were, out of due time.

The Spirit gives this inward, effectual call in many ways. Some, like Lydia, have been secretly allured to the Savior, and could not state the specific time or manner of the Spirit's gracious work. Others, like the Philippian jailer, have for a time, suffered the terrors of the Lord and been made to cry out, trembling and astonished, "What must I do to be saved?"

Often man-centered evangelism acts as if the success of the gospel is owing to the piety, the power of persuasion, or the elequence of those dispensing the gospel. But God-centered evangelism recognizes and acknowledges the absolute necessity of the effectual, inward call of the Spirit.

Man-centered evangelism ascribes the saving response to the gospel to man's will. God-centered evangelism knows to be true what the Bible clearly teaches, that no man can come to Christ except he is drawn (John 6:44). However, the Spirit's effectual work does no violence to the will. While the Spirit effectually draws sinners to Christ, He deals with them in a way that is agreeable to their rational nature *"so that they may come most freely, being made willing by His grace."* The liberty of the will is not invaded, for that would destroy its very nature; rather, its obstinacy is overcome; its perseverance removed; and the whole soul, powerfully, yet gently and sweetly, is attracted to the Savior. The compliance of the soul is voluntary, while the power of the Spirit is effectual and almighty. Psalm 110:3 expresses it beautifully: "Thy people shall be willing in the day of thy power. . . ."

God-centered evangelism says, only the Spirit can empower us for carrying out the commission to evangelize. This is very humbling to proud, self-satisfied evangelists. But, it is very hopeful and helpful to humble sowers of the seed, and also, very hopeful to poor helpless sinners. God can do something for them that they cannot do for themselves.

In order for sinners to benefit from the atoning work of Christ, that work has to be applied to them by the Holy Spirit. All that is necessary for salvation is accomplished in Christ's work, even the guarantee of its application. But what that means is that there is something so seriously wrong with the sinner that he will never accept Christ's freely-offered salvation, unless God the Spirit does something in the sinner himself — that something is called *regeneration* (John 3:3).

The free offer of the gospel meets with no success unless God, by His Spirit, does something for the sinner that he cannot do for himself. The failure of a saving response to the gospel is not because of any deficiency in the gospel, but because man is spiritually deaf, blind, and dead.

The Scriptures clearly teach us why sinners reject the gospel. It is not for lack of evidence or from intellectual doubt, but *always* because there is something dangerously and damningly wrong with the sinner's will. There must be a change in the sinner's *"willer."* That necessary change is what God does by His Spirit in the sinner. This is called *"regeneration," "the new birth,"* being *"born from above,"* etc.

Regeneration and conversion are *not* the same thing, though they are unquestionably so intimately related that it is difficult, if not impossible, to separate them in time and in our experience. It should not surprise us therefore, that regeneration and conversion are often confused.

True conversion always follows regeneration. Yet, the Scriptures clearly teach that regeneration is wholly the work of God the Spirit changing the heart *(mind, affections, will)*: "In whom also we have obtained an inheritance, being predestinated according to the purpose of him who worketh all things *after the counsel of his own will*" (Eph. 1:11).

Conversion is the *act of man* turning toward God in faith and repentance because of that powerful change that is wrought in his heart by the Holy Spirit.

Many biblical terms and expressions teach the idea of *begetting:*

> Being born again [begotten], not of corruptible seed, but of incorruptible seed, by the Word of God, which liveth and abideth for ever (I Peter 1:23).

> Not by works of righteousness which we have done, but according to his mercy he saved us, by the washing of regeneration, and renewing of the Holy Ghost (Titus 3:5).

> Of his own will *begat* he us with the word of truth, that we should be a kind of first-fruits of his creatures (James 1:18).

To *quicken* or *make alive* is another term used to express this internal work of God the Spirit. Many times, if not most, in the Scriptures, the works of regeneration and conversion are included under the one term *"regeneration"* because God is operative from the beginning to the end. However, because He is continually operative does not prove that He does not operate differently in one part from what He does in the other.

And in our understanding, it is important to have this difference made clear. Our understanding on this point will affect our *methods* in evangelism, that is, whether they are man-centered or God-centered. Our understanding here will show us the cause of conversion, and thus we will lay the crown at God's feet, and we will give Him the glory for our salvation. We will not brag about our big decision as the cause, but rather, we will know that *"our decision," "our faith," "our repentance"* are *results* of what God did in that powerful, gracious work of *regeneration.* We will understand that hymn writer who wrote, "I am a debtor to mercy *alone.*"

Let me try to illustrate this by a rather homely illustration. If you shoot a bullet through a board and someone asks you which comes first, the bullet or the hole, in time and experience, you would have a hard time separating the bullet from the hole. But in your understanding, you would be very clear as to the cause. The power and the cause was the bullet — the result was the hole.

Regeneration is solely the work of God — faith and repentance are the results; therefore, men believe and repent because they are born again. Yet we may not be able to discern in time or in our experience any separation between the new birth and conversion. This is the biblical, God-centered view.

If men were to believe in order to be born again, we would have to lay the crown for salvation at man's feet. That would be a reward for believing, and would therefore be man-centered.

The Bible teaches that God operates immediately upon the heart to prepare the way for truth. From the biblical description of man's spiritual condition, this is evident:

1. He is spiritually dead (Eph. 2:1): "And you hath he quickened, who were dead in trespasses and sins."
2. He is spiritually blind (Eph. 4:18): "Having the understanding darkened, being alienated from the life of God through the ignorance that is in them, because of the blindness of their heart."
3. He is enslaved to sin (John 8:34): "Jesus answered them, Verily, verily, I say unto you, Whosoever committeth sin is the servant of sin." (Rom. 6:17, 18): "But God be thanked, that ye were the servants of sin, but ye have obeyed from the heart that form of doctrine which was delivered you. Being then made free from sin, ye became the servants of righteousness."
4. He needs deliverance from the powers of darkness (Col. 1:13): "Who hath delivered us from the power

48

of darkness, and hath translated us into the kingdom of His dear Son."

5. The natural man is incapable of knowing or discerning the things of the Spirit (I Cor. 2:14): "But
the natural man receiveth not the things of the Spirit
of God: for they are foolishness unto him: neither
can he know them, because they are spiritually discerned."

6. The natural man is incapable of changing himself
(Jer. 13:23): "Can the Ethiopian change his skin, or
the leopard his spots? then may ye also do good,
that are accustomed to do evil."

7. He is defiled in conscience (Titus 1:15, 16): "Unto
the pure all things are pure: but unto them that are
defiled and unbelieving is nothing pure; but even
their mind and conscience is defiled. They profess
that they know God; but in works they deny him,
being adominable, and disobedient, and unto every
good work reprobate."

These passages show man to be in a condition from which
he must be rescued even to understand and appreciate the
truth of God.

The work of the Spirit in regeneration is subjective, that
is, His influence in man's life. The Spirit's initial subjective
work is *regeneration,* and without this work, no man can see
the kingdom of God (John 3:3). No preacher, regardless of
his training, preparation, eloquence, subtlety of wit, or
power of persuasion can regenerate one soul; and if man is
not regenerated, he will not believe or repent. This point
alone would change most of our evangelistic methods and
would even change our language as we call sinners.

You ask, "How would it change our language and our invitation?" Well, if God must do something before the sinner can do anything, spiritually, then we would plead with
sinners to call on Jesus to do something *for* them instead of

49

begging these "powerful sinners" to do something *with* Jesus. We would insist that sinners take the posture of the poor leper in Luke 5:12—"And it came to pass, when he was in a certain city, behold a man full of leprosy: who seeing Jesus fell on his face, and besought him, saying, Lord, *if thou wilt,* thou canst make me clean"—or, the posture of blind Bartimeus—"Oh thou Son of David have mercy on me"—or the poor publican in Luke 18—"God be merciful to me a sinner." When we command sinners to repent (". . . but God commandeth all men everywhere to repent. . . , " Acts 17:30) we are commanding them to do what the natural man will not or cannot do apart from God doing something. "Him hath God exalted with his right hand, for to *give* repentance to Israel and forgiveness of sins."

When we command men to believe on the name of Christ ("And this is his commandment, that we should believe on the name of his Son Jesus Christ . . . , " I John 3:23) we are commanding them to do what no natural man can do apart from God doing something. My point is to show the biblical principle of boxing sinners up to the mercy and power of God; the principle of *bowing*, not bargaining. This exalts God and puts sinners in the dust.

Properly handled, this is not discouraging to sinners but very encouraging and hopeful. There is a powerful and merciful God in heaven who is ready, able, and willing to do for poor deaf, blind, dead sinners what they cannot do for themselves. This is hope.

When Jesus says a man must be born again, he presupposes that he is spiritually dead. When the apostle Paul speaks of the Christian as a *"new creature,"* he indicates no spiritual life; thus God must make something *new — a new creation.*

If there is a *"new birth"* or a *"new creation,"* this must be from a source outside of the one born or created; there must be a birth from above. A corpse cannot make any contribution to its life.

Intellectual arguments will do no good for a dead man. You can try the sugar approach or the vinegar approach; you can entice him by the sweet promise of love and forgiveness; or thunder in his ears about the majesty of God, Mount Sinai and the threats of hell, or you can sit down with him night after night showing him the logic and beauty of the gospel. But if the Holy Spirit does not give him *spiritual life*, he cannot and will not savingly respond to the gospel.

Neither is there any value in using physical threats. Rome never won a soul to Christ by use of fire, the sword, the hangman's noose or the torture rack. One of David Livingstone's first converts was an African chief, Sechale, who thought he could make his tribesman believe by force. So he suggested one day to Livingstone, "I shall call my head man, and with our whips of rhinoceros hide, we will soon make them all believe together." He did not realize that the natural man is dead spiritually, and that a rhinoceros-hide whip cannot make a man believe; only the Holy Spirit can do so. Whips cannot touch the soul; only man's skin. Jesus said, "Do not be afraid of those who kill the body but cannot kill the soul" (Matt. 10:28).

All these things then, show us man's great need for the regenerating work of the Holy Spirit. There are no degrees in regeneration — a man is regenerated or he is not. Regeneration happens in a split second. A man is either dead or he is alive.

In Acts 16:14, we have the record of Lydia's conversion. Note the order. She heard Paul preach; the Lord opened her heart; then she heeded the things which were spoken by Paul. Between hearing and heeding, *God did something* — "the Lord opened her heart."

"Well," we ask, "what are the results of regeneration?"

Although we cannot see the wind, we can see its results. Likewise in regeneration, we may not know how the Holy

Spirit operates, but we can observe the results.

The beauty of it all is that man's power is not powerful enough to resist the Spirit's saving work. The power of grace is greater than the power of the will of an unregenerate man. So none are too far gone for the Holy Spirit.

If there is anything we need today in evangelism, it is the power of the Holy Spirit. Oh, for that heavenly Dove to come and regenerate poor, dead sinners. Without the regenerating work of the Holy Spirit, there will be no success at winning souls, regardless of the man-made machinery and feverish activities. Therefore, above all, pray for the regenerating influence of the Holy Spirit.

Jesus said, "If ye then, being evil, know how to give good gifts unto your children: how much more shall your heavenly Father give the Holy Spirit to them that ask him?" (Luke 11:13).

A man must be regenerated in order to believe, and only the Spirit can do that powerful, miraculous work in the heart of the sinner.

6. WHAT IS THE DIFFERENCE?

To the law and to the testimony: if they speak not according to this word, it is because there is no light in them.

— Isaiah 8:20

In considering God-centered and man-centered evangelism, we ask again, What is the difference?

The short answer is, *theology*. Immediately, eyebrows go up, and we hear someone say, "We don't need any of this theology talk; just tell people about Jesus." That sounds very pious and simple, but *which* Jesus should we tell them about — the *"Jehovah's Witness Jesus,"* the *"Mormon Jesus,"* the *"Christian Science Jesus,"* or one of a thousand other Christs on the religious market?

Well, just as soon as you begin to describe the Christ of the Bible, you are into theology, and everyone who believes in God and in Jesus Christ has a theology, though not always true biblical theology. Therefore, before you oversimplify the subject, let me give a brief statement as to what *theology* is.

Theology is a study or belief of God and His relationship to the world of man. It is a rational interpretation of the Christian faith, practice and experience.

The branches of theology in particular that make the difference between God-centered and man-centered evangelism are in five areas, all vitally related to evangelism and related to each other.

FIRST THEOLOGICAL DIFFERENCE

The *first* area of theological difference is the condition of man.

If man is spiritually deaf, spiritually blind, and spiritually dead, then *God must do something* before man can hear, see, or live, and thus God will receive *all* the glory for man's salvation.

If, on the other hand, man is just sick and not dead, he only needs God's help, and he must divide the glory between himself and the help God gives.

What we believe about the condition of man will have a profound effect upon the message and methods we employ to rescue him.

SECOND THEOLOGICAL DIFFERENCE

The *second* area of theological difference is what you believe about God's sovereign election. Again, do not let the word *election* frighten you. It is a good Bible word. Just take your concordance and look up the word and all its synonyms: *foreknew, chosen,* etc. Both God-centered and man-centered evangelism believe in election because it is in the Bible. The difference lies in what they believe about it.

Man-centered evangelism may have one of several theories, such as: Election consists in the choice of whole nations, which choice however, relates purely to their privileged condition in this world, and not to their collective eternal state in another world.

Other man-centered theories assert that:

1. Salvation of individuals is the result of their own choice and perseverance.
2. The election made by God is simply an election of a class.
3. So far as the election of individuals took place in eternity, it was only as God foresaw what would be the result of the election of a class.

4. Election is made upon condition that some would accept the offer of the gospel.

God-centered evangelism also believes in election because it is taught in the Bible, but God-centered evangelism believes what the Bible teaches about it, namely, that election is, in the words of Dr. James P. Boyce:[1]

 a. An act of God, and not the result of the choice of the elect.

  The following passages are sufficient, though the examples are far more numerous.

  John 13:18 — "I know whom I have chosen."

  John 15:16 — "Ye did not choose me, but I chose you."

  Rom. 8:33 — "Who shall lay anything to the charge of God's chosen ones?"

  Rom. 9:15 — "I will have mercy on whom I will have mercy."

  Eph. 1:4 — "Even as he chose us in him."

  Eph. 1:11 — "Having been foreordained according to the purpose of him who worketh all things after the counsel of his will."

  II Thes. 2:13 — "God chose you from the beginning unto salvation."

 b. That this choice is one of individuals, not of classes.

  Acts 13:48 — "As many as were ordained to eternal life believed." This is a historical statement made subsequent to the event, not by man's knowledge but by inspiration.

  Eph. 1:4, 5 — "Even as he chose us in him . . . having foreordained us unto adoption as sons."

---

[1] *Abstract of Systematic Theology,* Dr. James P. Boyce, Chap. XXIX, "Election."

II Thes. 2:13 — "But we are bound to give thanks to God always for you, brethren, beloved of the Lord, for that God chose you from the beginning unto salvation in sanctification of the Spirit and belief of the truth."

c. That it is by the good pleasure of God.

John 6:37, 39, 44, 64, 65 — "All that which the Father giveth me shall come unto me. . . . This is the will of him that sent me, that of all that which he hath given me I should lose nothing. . . . No man can come to me except the Father which sent me draw him. . . . Jesus knew from the beginning who they were that believed not, and who it was that should betray him. And he said, for this cause have I said unto you, that no man can come unto me, except it be given unto him of the Father."

John 15:16 — "Ye did not choose me, but I chose you, and appointed you, that ye should go and bear fruit." The object to be attained cannot be the cause.

John 17:2 — "As thou gavest him authority over all flesh, that whatsoever thou hast given him to them he should give eternal life." See also vvs. 6-12.

Acts 22:14 — Ananias says to Paul, "The God of our fathers hath appointed thee to know his will."

Eph. 1:5 — In the fourth verse having referred to God's choice of us before the foundation of the world, he says in this fifth, "Having foreordained us unto adoption as sons through Jesus Christ unto himself, according to the good pleasure of his will, to the praise of the glory of his grace." In verse 11, we are said to be predestinated to our inheritance "according to the purpose of him who worketh all things after the counsel of his will."

James 1:18 — "Of his own will he brought us forth by the word of truth."

d. That it is according to an eternal purpose.

Jer. 1:5 — "Before I formed thee in the belly, I knew thee, and before thou camest forth out of the womb, I sanctified thee."

Mt. 25:34 — "Then shall the King say unto them on his right hand, Come, ye blessed of my Father, inherit the kingdom prepared for you from the foundation of the world."

Eph. 1:4 — "Even as he chose us in him before the foundation of the world."

II Thes. 2:13 — "But we are bound to give thanks to God always for you, brethren, beloved of the Lord, for that God chose you from the beginning unto salvation in sanctification of the Spirit and belief of the truth."

II Tim. 1:9 — "Who saved us, and called us with a holy calling, not according to our works, but according to his own purpose and grace, which was given us in Christ Jesus before time eternal.

e. That it is an election to salvation, and not to outward privilege.

John 10:26 — "Ye believe not, because ye are not of my sheep." Verse 27—"My sheep hear my voice, and I know them, and they follow me."

Rom. 8:28–30 — "We know that to them that love God all things work together for good, even to them that are called according to his purpose." Paul now proceeds to tell who these are. "For whom he foreknew, he also foreordained to be conformed to the image of his Son, that he might be the first-born among many brethren: and whom he foreordained, them he also called: and whom he called, them he also justified: and whom he

57

justified, them he also glorified.''

The God-centered view holds that God, of His own purpose, has from eternity determined to save a definite number of mankind, from every tribe, tongue, and nation, as individuals, not for any merit or work of theirs, or any value to Him of them, but by His own good pleasure. The *Abstract of Principles*[2] puts it like this:

> Election is God's eternal choice of persons unto
> everlasting life — not because of foreseen merit
> in them, but of His mere mercy in Christ. . . .

Again, your view of this important doctrine will have a profound effect on both the message and methods of evangelism.

THIRD THEOLOGICAL DIFFERENCE

The *third* area of theological truth that will reveal whether evangelism is God-centered or man-centered is what you believe about the atonement of Christ. Just what happened at the cross? What did Christ accomplish? And, how is that which He accomplished applied in time?

1. Did He die savingly for all the sins of *all* men?

    or

2. Did He die savingly for *all* the sins of some men?

    or

3. Did He die for some of the sins of *all* men?

    or

4. Did He just die to make salvation possible and now stands idly by, waiting for man's decision?

---

[2]The Abstract of Principles, which was written into the charter of Southern Seminary on April 30, 1858, at which Institution every professor commits himself ". . . to teach in accordance with and not contrary to the Abstract of Principles . . ."; Mueller, *History of Southern Seminary* (Broadman Press), p. 238.

If the first is true, why are not all men free from the punishment due them for their sins? You answer, "because of unbelief." I ask, "Is this unbelief a sin, or is it not? Then Christ suffered the punishment for this unbelief. And if he did, why must that hinder them more than their other sins for which He died? If he did not die for this sin of unbelief, then He did not die for all their sins."

If the third were true, all men would have some sins to answer for and no one would be saved.

If the fourth were true, no one would be saved because without the powerful work of the Spirit, men will *always* make the wrong decision.

Therefore, the second is the true biblical view. Christ suffered for all the sins of all His sheep in the whole world, and none of them will be lost. This view will make the difference between God-centered and man-centered evangelism.

> He shall see of the travail of his soul, and shall be *satisfied:* by his knowledge shall my righteous servant justify *many;* for he shall bear their iniquities (Isa. 53:11).

> But ye believe not, *because ye are not my sheep,* as I said unto you. My sheep hear my voice, and I know *them*, and *they* follow me. And I give unto *them* eternal life and *they* shall never perish, neither shall any man pluck *them* out of my hand (John 10:26–28).

FOURTH THEOLOGICAL DIFFERENCE

The *fourth* area of biblical theology that will determine whether you have a God-centered or man-centered evangelism is what you believe about the Holy Spirit in the application of what Christ accomplished on the cross.

For example, if you believe that man has enough power to resist God almighty's power to save, that is, to resist His purpose in sending His Son, your evangelism will be man-centered. On the other hand, if you believe that God almighty's power is such that He can overpower man's will in such a way as to cause sinners willingly to come to Him — your evangelism will be God-centered (Ps. 110:3).

Man-centered evangelism believes that God votes for you, the devil votes against you, and you cast the deciding vote.

Of course, anyone who thinks through that idea will see that if that were true, then God would not have any more power than the devil because they are deadlocked, and that means that you are more powerful than either God or the devil.

The God-centered view rejects this unbiblical view and believes what the Bible teaches, "The Lord opened Lydia's heart" (Acts 16:14). "Whom God foreloved, He also did predestinate, them He also called; and whom He called, them He also justified; and whom He justified, them He also glorified"; and He lost none in-between (Rom. 8:28–33).

The God-centered view is that God first loved His own and loved them so as to work powerfully in them by His Spirit, to convict, convince and convert them, and thus they attribute their salvation not to their vote or decision, but to God's powerful grace; and they can truly sing with understanding, "Amazing grace, how sweet the sound that saved a wretch like me." Not "amazing *decision*" (that is man-centered) but, "amazing *grace*" (that is God-centered). We love Him because He *first* loved us.

Therefore, God-centered evangelism represents all persons of the Trinity working together for the salvation of poor, lost sinners. What the Father planned in eternity, the Son purchased on the cross, and the Holy Spirit savingly applies in time. "He shall see of the travail of his soul, and shall be satisfied; by his knowledge shall my righteous servant justify many; for he shall bear their iniquities" (Isa. 53:11). Please note: He will be *satisfied*—not a failure, not frustrated, not disappointed—*satisfied*.

Man-centered evangelism has a frustrated Trinity. It has:

1. The Father planning the redemption of every individual.
2. The Son purchasing the redemption of all.
3. But, the Spirit savingly applying what the Father planned and the Son purchased only to *some*.

FIFTH THEOLOGICAL DIFFERENCE

The *fifth* area of theological difference is in respect to God's keeping power.

God-centered evangelism believes that God powerfully keeps those whom He saves in time.

> But ye believe not, because ye are not of my sheep, as I said unto you. My sheep hear my voice, and I know them, and they follow me. And I give unto them eternal life; and they shall never perish, neither shall any man pluck them out of my hand. My Father, which gave them me, is greater than all; and no man is able to pluck them out of my Father's hand (John 10:26–29).

> Who shall separate us from the love of Christ? shall tribulation, or distress, or persecution, or famine, or nakedness, or peril, or sword? As it is written, For thy sake we are killed all the day long; we are accounted as sheep for the slaughter. Nay, in all these things we are more than conquerors through him that loved us. For I am persuaded, that neither death, nor life, nor angels, nor principalities, nor powers, not things present, nor things to come, nor height, nor depth, nor any other creature, shall be able to separate us from the love of God, which is in Christ Jesus our Lord (Rom. 8:35–39).

THE EFFECTS OF THEOLOGY

How do these theological differences affect evangelism?

Because of an unbiblical theology, man-centered evangelism approaches sinners who are deaf, blind, dead and unwilling by trying to get them to do something *with* Jesus.

God-centered evangelism approaches sinners more like this:

> Oh, sinner, you are lost and my Bible tells me you are blind to spiritual things, and unless you are born of God, you cannot *see* the kingdom of God, let alone enter. Ah, sinner, it is worse than that. My Bible tells me you are dead in trespasses and sins — your only hope is in God who opens blinded eyes and who has power to raise the dead. Oh, sinner, there is a God in heaven who can make spiritually dead people alive. Call upon Him — cast yourself on His mercy. Take the posture of the poor leper (Luke 5:12): "And it came to pass, when he was in a certain city, behold a man was full of leprosy: who seeing Jesus fell on his face, and besought him, saying, Lord, *if thou wilt*, thou canst make me clean," or the poor publican with his plea for mercy, "God be merciful to me a sinner."

He is able, ready and willing to save all that come to Him by Jesus Christ.

God-centered evangelism, because of the biblical theology that undergirds it, stresses that faith is man's duty but is not within his ability. God gives what He commands or no one would be saved. Oh, blessed *"except"* found in John 6:44: "No man can come to me *except* the Father which hath sent me draw him: and I will raise him up at the last day." If it were not for that blessed *except*, every sinner would go to hell.

We learn from our Lord's prayer in John 17:2, that eternal life is a gift that is in the hands of a sovereign giver: "As thou hast given him power over all flesh, that he should give eternal life to as many as thou hast given him." This verse teaches where eternal life is — in the hands of a sovereign

Christ. And if men would believe that, they would do one of two things — *curse God, or bow at His feet,* and ask for what only God can give, eternal life.

Man-centered evangelism leads men to believe that they are saved by a decision. God-centered evangelism teaches that man's decision is a result of what God does by His Word and Spirit, and thus saved men lay the crown of their salvation at God's feet and not at their own, excluding all boasting. We see it in a passage like Psalm 110:3, "Thy people shall be made willing in the day of thy power." Or, in such pasages as Psalm 65:4, "Blessed is the man whom thou choosest, and causest to approach unto thee, that he may dwell in thy courts. . .," or I John 4:19, "We love him, *because He first* loved us." This great truth boxes sinners up to the mercy of God.

I remember hearing an old country preacher pick his guitar and sing a kind of "hillbilly" song, and I'm sure he did not understand the great theological truth that the song clearly set forth, that is, that *God makes man willing.* I'll call it the:

Hornet Song

When the Canaanites hardened their hearts against God,
   and grieved Him because of their sin,
God sent along hornets to bring them to terms,
   and to help His own people to win.

If a nest of live hornets were brought to this room,
   and the creatures allowed to go free,
You would not need urging to make yourself scarce,
   you'd want to get out, don't you see!

They would not lay hold and by force of their strength,
   throw you out of the window, oh, no!
They would not compel you to go against your will,
   but, they would just make you willing to go.

When Jonah was sent to the work of the Lord,
    the outlook was not very bright.
He never had done such a hard thing before,
    so he backed and ran off from the fight.

Now, the Lord sent a great fish to swallow him up,
    the story I am sure you all know.
God did not compel him to go against his will,
    but, He just made him willing to go.

    CHORUS:

God does not compel us to go, oh, no!
    He never compels us to go.
God does not compel us to go against our will,
    but, He just makes us willing to go.

This song is teaching the truth found in John 6:44, Psalm 110:3, and Psalm 65:4.

Now, at this point I think I hear someone ask, "But, doesn't the sinner cooperate in his salvation?" Well, if he did, he would have to take some of the credit, and salvation would not be by grace alone, but rather, it would be by grace and man's cooperation. And, we could not say with Jonah, "Salvation is of the Lord." We would have to say, "Salvation is of the Lord and man's cooperation." We could not sing, "We are debtors to mercy alone," or, "Amazing Grace."

Let me give you three New Testament pictures of conversion that show that salvation is not by God *and* cooperation.

1. In John 4: Jesus deals with a woman living in adultery. Surely, she was not cooperating with God. She had had five husbands, and was living with the sixth without benefit of clergy.

2. In Luke 19: We have a picture of a crooked tax collector, Zacchaeus, who was stealing everything that was loose at both ends. Surely, he was not cooperating with God.

3. In Acts 9: We have Saul of Tarsus, hating Christians,

locking them up in jail, hunting them down in every home in order to persecute them. Surely, he was not cooperating with God.

If anyone gets that harlot woman saved, it will have to be God. If anyone gets that thief and extortioner saved, it will have to be God. If anyone gets that evil persecutor and blasphemer saved, it will have to be God. Bless God! Salvation is of the Lord, and God saves sinners by grace and power.

Now this encouraging truth does not leave man passive or inert. The very opposite takes place. The Spirit does not kill man, or regard him as a tin can, or a piece of wood, or a robot. No! No! The Spirit graciously and powerfully takes possession of the man, lays hold of his whole being (mind, affection and will) for time and eternity. The Spirit does not annihilate man's powers, but renews his powerlessness. The Spirit does not destroy man's will, but frees it from sin. The Spirit does not stifle or obliterate man's conscience, but sets it free from darkness, and regenerates, recreates man in his entirety, and in renewing him by grace and power, causes him to love and consecrate himself to God most freely.

This is God-centered evangelism, and because of this, we say evangelism is a work of divine grace, divine power, and divine sovereignty.

No preacher or evangelist since the day of the apostle Paul ever laid so much stress on the absolute sovereignty of God as did that great soul-winner, Jonathan Edwards. And it may come as a surprise to the "Finneyism," man-centered evangelism of our day, to discover that the preaching of God's sovereignty was very fruitful. Under the ministry of Edwards, revival swept through his church. Let me quote the great evangelist himself on this point.

> I think that I have found that no discourses have been more remarkably blessed than those in which the Doctrines of God's absolute sovereignty, with regard to the

salvation of sinners were stressed.

God-centered evangelism is not some quick sales pitch or technique geared to the powerful sinner's decision. Preachers and personal workers are not salesmen, but communicators of God's eternal truth about Himself and the condition of poor, lost sinners. Nor are preachers politicans drumming up votes for Jesus. Jesus doesn't need any votes. He is already in office by God almighty's decree. Peter made this clear in his first sermon (Acts 2:36): "Therefore, let all the House of Israel know assuredly, that God hath made that same Jesus, whom ye have crucified, both Lord and Christ."

If you grasp this biblical truth, you will see that it is not so much the sinner moving and Christ standing impotently still, waiting for the sinner's decision, but rather Christ coming, seeking and finding the sinner. He visits them inwardly, making them willing, and by His Word and Spirit empowers them freely to come.

This is God-centered evangelism and is very hopeful to poor sinners, that there is a God in Heaven who can do for them what they cannot do for themselves.

It is also hopeful and encouraging to true gospel preachers to know that there is a sovereign God who is able to do for those to whom they preach what the preacher has no power to do for them, although he longs and prays to see it done.

Do you not see that God-centered evangelism therefore is lifting up Christ before men as one who has power to unstop deaf ears, open blinded eyes, and raise the spiritually dead?

God-centered evangelism is more concerned with God, and therefore, wants to bring glory to God. The main beam of God-centered evangelism, therefore, teaches men to worship God.

Man-centered evangelism aims at making man feel better. God-centered evangelism makes man feel better, by first giving him a right view of God and His ways with man.

I would appeal to any serious reader to study the evangelism of the great soul winners, such as, Spurgeon, Bunyan, Whitefield, and Edwards, and you will soon see that it was God-centered — a *God-honoring message and God-honoring methods* that were consistent with the message.

But, my greatest appeal would be to the sacred manual of evangelism, that is, the Book of Acts. Study carefully the methods employed by the apostolic preachers and their successors.

Before moving to the methods of evangelism, let me give a concise summary of the message of evangelism. The message is the gospel, a word with so many meanings that it hardly has any specific meaning.

The gospel in its large and general meaning is:

1. The teachings of Christ and His apostles.
2. Sometimes the history of Christ's birth, life, resurrection and ascension.
3. Sometimes the preaching of the Word of Christ, particularly, the doctrines of Christ, and the offer of salvation through Him.

The gospel in its strict and proper meaning signifies *good news, glad tidings, joyful announcement.* Dr. John Brown, senior minister of the United Presbyterian Congregation and Professor of Exegetical Theology, gave the best concise, succinct, comprehensive definition of the gospel that I have ever read or heard.[3] I quote,

> The Saxon word "Gospel", like the Greek word of which it is a literal translation, signifies agreeable intelligence, a joyful announcement, good news, glad tidings; and is, in the New Testament, ordinarily em-

---

[3] *The Resurrection of Life; An Exposition of First Corinthians XV,* pp. 7, 8.

ployed as a descriptive designation of the revelation of Divine mercy to our lost world, — the divinely-inspired account of the only way in which guilty, depraved, and miserable men may be delivered from sin and its consequences, obtain the Divine approbation and favour, be raised to the true dignity and excellence of their intellectual and moral nature, in the knowledge of God, and conformity to his mind and will, and be made happy in all the variety, and to the full extent, of their capacities of enjoyment, and during the whole eternity of their being, by the free grace of God, and through the redemption that is in Christ Jesus. The sum and substance of that revelation is contained in the statement made by the apostle in the third and fourth verses of this chapter, — "that Christ died for our sins according to the Scriptures; and was buried, and rose again from the dead on the third day, according to the Scriptures."

This divinely-inspired message has four main ingredients:[4]

First, it is a message about God, our Creator and Judge, and His absolute claims on us as creatures.

Second, it is a message about sin. And, what is sin? "Sin is the transgression of the law" (I John 4:7). "For where no law is there is no transgression" (Rom. 4:15). "By the law is the knowledge of sin" (Rom. 3:20).

Third, it is a message about Christ: who He is, why He came, what He did, why he did it, where He is now, and His coming again—but, particularly, how He is the only Mediator between God and man, and how sinners are reconciled to God by His person and work.

Fourth, it is a summons of faith and repentance: ". . .the time is fulfilled, and the kingdom of God is at hand: repent

---

[4]See J. I. Packer, *Evangelism and the Sovereignty of God.*

ye, and believe the gospel" (Mark 1:15). "Testifying both to the Jews, and also to the Greeks, repentance toward God, and faith toward our Lord Jesus Christ" (Acts 20:21).

7. METHODS OF INVITING SINNERS TO CHRIST

Now we begin to consider God-centered methods. The biblical method is always God-centered and God-honoring. Before we actually examine the New Testament as to God-centered methods, we should have a clear idea of some of the language that is used in evangelism.

The expression "come to Christ" is a good one, but it is surrounded by much ignorance and confusion when it is made part of wrong methods of evangelism. What does that expression mean to its hearers? Surely it is necessary for sinners to come to Christ in order to be saved. But when a preacher calls sinners to the front of a church, while the congregation sets the mood by means of an "invitational hymn," it is likely that most hearers will equate coming to Christ with "coming forward" or "walking the aisle."

If questioned about the matter, the preacher might say "walking an aisle" does not save. Yet, at the same time, by his very language and methods, he is equating coming forward with "coming to Christ," and thus, many poor souls are deceived.

We should all want to examine our methods by the Scriptures. It may come as a surprise to many sincere men that there is not one line of Scripture to support this man-made system. Not only is it not in the Bible, but it was never practiced in the church (any church) for the first eighteen hundred years. Let me emphasize again, it was not practiced by our Lord, or His apostles, or the early church. It was never practiced in the church until sometime between 1830 and

1850, when a man by the name of Charles G. Finney (who was defrocked from the Presbyterian church on doctrinal charges) started it with what he called "the inquiry room" and "the anxious seat." I often wonder how some people think a sinner got saved in the first eighteen hundred years of the church without this man-made system. Please bear in mind, I am not talking about *invitations,* (that is, inviting sinners to the Savior). If a preacher does not invite sinners to Christ, he had better quit preaching! I am talking about this man-made, man-centered, unbiblical *method* of invitation. This invitation system has deceived and confused millions of people and continues to do so.

Let me plead with you to search the Scriptures on this point. Let me also beg you to study church history for its practice. You say, "What is it based on? Why is it a touchstone of orthodoxy in many churches?" It started with Finney's Pelagian, or semi-Pelagian theology. Therefore, it is based on unbiblical theology.

There are two Scriptures that are usually used to support some physical or overt response. One is Matthew 4:19: ". . . follow me and I will make you fishers of men. . . ." This passage is not even talking about his hearer's salvation but of their winning others to Christ. The disciples left their nets and literally and physically followed Jesus, but Jesus is not physically with us now. And, if a preacher stood on the dock of some fishing marina today and said, "Follow Jesus," he would not mean something physical. What does "following Jesus" mean? Following Jesus is learning His teachings, living under the influence of those teachings, and applying His teachings to everyday life and practice. Even in the days of His flesh, a physical response may have been the case sometimes, but the meaning of "Come unto Me" or "Follow Me" was a spiritual identification with Him by faith and repentance. This was clearly the fundamental sense of His words "Follow Me" and "Come unto Me." Therefore,

Matthew 4:19 is not a valid Scripture to use to support this man-centered, man-invented invitation system.

The second Scripture that is often used to support this system is Matthew 10:32, 33: "Whosoever therefore shall confess me before men, him will I confess also before my Father which is in heaven. But whosoever shall deny me before men, him will I also deny before my Father which is in heaven."

Just what is our Lord saying? Look carefully at His words. Is our Lord simply teaching that by the act of physical confession we become Christians, or is He teaching that the one indispensable mark of those who are Christians is that they will confess and live a life that openly acknowledges Him? The answer is crystal clear. To confess Christ is the spiritual duty of every Christian; confessing is not how to become a Christian. One must be in possession of Christ before he can confess Him. It is clear that Jesus is not telling sinners how to make a decision, or the way the new birth takes place. No, No! He is teaching that confessing Him before men is the spiritual duty of Christians. Any honest examination of the text will agree with this interpretation. Therefore, this text cannot be used to support this man-centered, man-made invitation system.

If anyone would take a cursory glance at the sacred manual of evangelism (the Book of Acts), he would see the apostolic example at its purest. Ask the questions as you read the Book of Acts: What did they say and do at the end of their sermons? How was confession made? The answer will be clear—baptism of those who believed. And, there never was any overt act equated with coming to Christ.

Someone may ask, "Why waste time on such a subject. It works, doesn't it?" Yes, men are saved where the system is practiced, but, they are saved by the truth that the Spirit uses, not because of the unbiblical system. My reason for raising the issue is that many men, women, boys and girls

73

are deceived, and to be deceived about your own salvation is the worst kind of deception.

My second reason for pleading an examination of this system is that many sincere preachers and evangelists have never examined this system, neither from the Scriptures nor from history.

I have questioned some of these sincere men who practice this system and their usual answer is, "It works!" To ask if it works is not the right question. The right questions are *Is it true?* and *Is it biblical?*

This is not an uncharitable attack on any personalities that practice this system, because some of the most godly and respected men in the ministry use this unbiblical system. However, what they do not seem to know is that it was through their preaching of the Christ of the Bible that many were saved under their ministry, and these would have been saved without using this man-centered, unbiblical system, which has contributed to the deception of millions. Let me, therefore, make a sincere plea for a biblical and historical examination of this system.

That great preacher and soul winner whom all evangelicals love and respect, *Charles Haddon Spurgeon,* saw this system as it was beginning to emerge in his day and sounded a clarion warning concerning it. Hear the warning as I quote from the prince of preachers:[1]

> Let me say, very softly and whisperingly, that there are little things among ourselves which must be carefully looked after, or we shall have a leaven of Ritualism and priesthood working in our measures of meal. In our revival services, it might be as well to vary our procedure. Sometimes shut up that enquiry-room. I have my fears about that institution if it be used in

---

[1] C. H. Spurgeon, "The Minister in These Times," *An All Round Ministry* (Banner of Truth), p. 372.

permanence, and as an inevitable part of the services. It may be a very wise thing to invite persons who are under concern of soul to come apart from the rest of the congregation, and have conversation with godly people; but if you should ever see a notion is fashioning itself that there is something to be got in the private room which is not to be had at once in the assembly, or that God is more at that penitent form than elsewhere, aim a blow at that notion at once. We must not come back by a rapid march to the old ways of altars and confessionals, and have a Romish trumpery restored in a coarser form. If we make men think that conversation with ourselves or with our helpers is essential to their faith in Christ, we are taking the direct line for priestcraft. In the Gospel, the sinner and the Saviour are to come together, with none between. Speak upon this point very clearly. "You, sinner, sitting where you are, believing on the Lord Jesus Christ, shall have eternal life. Do not stop till you pass into an enquiry room. Do not think it essential to confer with me. Do not suppose that I have the keys of the Kingdom of Heaven, or that these godly men and women associated with me can tell you any other Gospel than this. He that believeth on the Son hath everlasting life."

What Spurgeon feared and warned against has come to pass!

Another quote from that great soul-winner, on his dealing with sinners:

Go home alone, [he would say,] "trusting in Jesus". [Spurgeon now quotes the sinner] "I would like to go into the enquiry room." "I dare say you would, but we are not willing to pander to popular superstition. We fear that in those rooms men are warmed into fictitious confidence. Very few of the supposed converts of enquiry rooms turn out well. Go to your God at

once, even where you are now. Cast yourself on
Christ, now, at once, ere you stir an inch!''

A recurring warning in his later sermons was:

God has not appointed salvation by enquiry rooms.
. . . For the most part, a wounded conscience, like a
wounded stag, delights to be alone that it may bleed in
secret.

FOUR DANGERS

There are four dangers of this man-made, Pelagian
system:

1. It conveys to sinners a condition of salvation that is
   not in the Bible and was never practiced or approved by Christ and His apostles.
2. To call sinners to the front of a church is not a divine
   command, but many times those who do not go forward are led to believe that they are not obeying the
   Spirit and, therefore, not obeying God. This is
   false, psychological guilt because no such thing was
   ever commanded by God or practiced in the New
   Testament. On the other hand, those who do go
   forward are often commended and are led to believe
   that they did something commendable, when in
   many cases, they have only added to their religious
   deception.
3. This unbiblical system has produced the greatest
   record of false statistics ever compiled by church or
   business.
4. This system has spawned the error of representing
   the faith in Christ as something to be done in order
   to salvation.

One of the most beautiful invitations given by our Lord is
found in Matthew 11:28–30. His hearers had already

gathered around Him physically, when He said, "Come unto me, all ye that labour and are heavy laden. . . ." Obviously, He was not talking about physical tiredness, or physically coming, because in the context He said, ". . . learn of me . . . and ye shall find rest unto your souls." Please note: finding rest by *learning of Him* is not some physical or overt act.

Our Lord, in John 6:35 said, ". . .I am the bread of life: he that cometh to me shall never hunger; and he that believeth on me shall never thirst." The test is clear that *coming* is eating, and *believing* is drinking, but surely not literally or physically. Again, our appeal is Holy Scriptures, not tradition.

> Is coming to Christ a physical or overt act?
> Is coming to Christ only a mental act?
> Is coming to Christ only a volitional act?
> Is coming to Christ some sort of mystical act, unfounded on truth?

The short answer to all four questions is *no*. Coming to Christ is *not* a physical or overt act. No, it is *not* only a mental act. No, it is *not* only a volitional act. And, no, it is *not* some mystical act unfounded on truth.[2]

This is one of the things that made David Brainerd, that great missionary, angry with God when he was under conviction. Actually, there were four things in the Bible that irritated him. Please note item 3 below pertaining to "coming to Christ."

> Thus, scores of times, I vainly imagined myself humbled and prepared for saving mercy. And while I was in this distressed, bewildered, and tumultuous

---

[2]The answer to these questions was well handled in a published sermon by Pastor Albert N. Martin some years ago. I am using the outline of this message as to what is involved in coming to Christ.

state of mind, the corruption of my heart was especially irritated with the following things:

1. *The strictness of the divine law.* For I found it was impossible for me, after my utmost pains, to answer its demands. I often made new resolutions, and as often broke them. I imputed the whole to carelessness and the want of being more watchful, and used to call myself a fool for my negligence. But when, upon a stronger resolution, and greater endeavors, and close application to fasting and prayer, I found all attempts fail; then I quarreled with the law of God, as unreasonably rigid. I thought if it extended only to my outward actions and behaviors I could bear with it; but I found it condemned me for my evil thoughts and sins of my heart, which I could not possibly prevent.

   I was extremely loth to own my utter helplessness in this matter: but after repeated disappointments, thought that, rather than perish, I could do a little more still; especially if such and such circumstances might but attend my endeavors and strivings. I hoped that I should strive more earnestly than ever if the matter came to extremity—though I never could find the time to do my utmost, in the manner I intended—and this hope of future more favorable circumstances, and of doing something great hereafter, kept me from utter despair in myself and from seeing myself fallen into the hands of a sovereign God, and dependent on nothing but free and boundless grace.

2. Another thing was, that *faith alone was the condition of salvation;* that God would not come down to lower terms and that He would not promise life and salvation upon my sincere and hearty prayers and endeavors. That word, Mark 16:16, "He that be-

lieveth not, shall be damned,'' cut off all hope there. I found faith was the sovereign gift of God, that I could not get it as of myself, and could not oblige God to bestow it upon me by any of my performances (Eph. 2:1–8). This, I was ready to say, is a hard saying, who can bear it? I could not bear that all I had done should stand for mere nothing, who had been very conscientious in duty, had been exceeding religious a great while, and had, as I thought, done much more than many others who had obtained mercy.

I confessed indeed the vileness of my duties; but then, what made them at that time seem vile was my wandering thoughts in them; not because I was all over defiled like a devil, and the principle corrupt from whence they flowed, so that I could not possibly do anything that was good. And therefore I called what I did, by the name of honest faithful endeavors; and could not bear it that God had made no promises of salvation to them.

3. Another thing was that *I could not find out what faith was;* or what it was to believe and come to Christ. I read the calls of Christ to the weary and heavy laden; but could find no way that He directed them to come in. I thought I would gladly come if I knew how, though the path of duty were ever so difficult. I read Mr. Stoddard's *Guide to Christ,* (which I trust was, in the hand of God, the happy means of my conversion), and my heart rose against the author; for though he told me my very heart all along under convictions, and seemed to be very beneficial to me in his directions; yet here he failed, he did not tell me anything I could do that would bring me to Christ, but left me as it were with a great gulf between, without any direction to get through.

For I was not yet effectually and experimentally taught that there could be no way prescribed whereby a natural man could, of his own strength, obtain that which is supernatural and which the highest angel cannot give.

4. Another thing to which I found a great inward opposition was the *sovereignty of God.* I could not bear that it should be wholly at God's pleasure, to save or damn me, just as He would. That passage, Romans 9:11–23, was a constant vexation to me, especially verse 21. Reading or meditating on this always destroyed my seeming good frames. For when I thought I was almost humbled and almost resigned, this passage would make my enmity against the sovereignty of God appear. When I came to reflect on my inward enmity and blasphemy, which arose on this occasion, I was the more afraid of God and driven further from any hopes of reconciliation with Him. It gave me such a dreadful view of myself that I dreaded more than ever to see myself in God's hands, at His sovereign disposal, and it made me more opposite than ever to submit to His sovereignty for I thought God designed my damnation.[3]

What does it mean to *"come to Christ"?* This sounds like a simple question. But, there is no simple answer. In fact, the best we can do is to show from the Scriptures what is involved in coming to Christ.

WHAT IS INVOLVED IN COMING TO CHRIST?
The first thing involved in coming to Christ is that there must be a *recognition* of a spiritual need. Though we must

---

[3]Jonathan Edwards, *The Life and Diary of David Brainerd,* (Moody Press), pp. 63–66.

not make this the warrant of faith, or the condition of coming, nevertheless, the recognition of a spiritual need is involved in coming to Christ. We must not make any kind of preparationism part of the warrant to come to Christ. Here is the warrant — whosoever will may come. Believe on the Lord Jesus Christ and thou shalt be saved. But, who does, in fact, come and savingly believe?

Let me give three familiar biblical invitations:

1. *Matthew 11:28:* Hear our Lord invite sinners:

> Come unto me . . . [who?] . . . all ye that labour and are heavy laden. . . .

All are invited, but who, in fact, wants rest for their souls? Only the *weary and heavy laden* — those who *feel a need.*

2. *Isaiah 55:1:* An Old Testament invitation:

> Ho, every one that thirsteth, come ye to the waters, and he that hath no money; come ye, buy, and eat; yea, come, buy wine and milk without money and without price.

"Come ye to the waters" means all may be invited, but who, in fact, comes? Only *thirsty people*, those who *recognize a need.*

3. *Revelation 22:17:* The last invitation in the Bible:

> And the Spirit and the bride say, Come. And let him that heareth say, Come. And let him that is athirst come. And whosoever will, let him take the water of life freely.

Many misquote this verse and use it to prove "whosoever will may come." If you examine this invitation closely and just read what is there, it does not say, "whosoever will may come," but, "whosoever will let him take the water of life freely." Who wants water? The answer is in the verse: "And let him that is *athirst* come."

Yes, we are to preach the gospel to every creature, and we

must freely offer the gospel to whosoever will. But, again I ask, *Who, in fact, will,* in a world of whosoever will-nots? Those who *recognize a spiritual need.* Thus, the first thing involved in "coming to Christ" is the recognition of a spiritual need.

The second thing involved in "coming to Christ" is a *revelation* of Christ to the heart as the only one suitable to meet that spiritual need. This is the greatest problem with Sunday morning Christianity — a host of people gathered at the eleven o'clock hour, going through externals of religion, trying to worship a Christ who has never been revealed to their hearts.

In Matthew 16:13–17, we see the necessity of the revelation of Christ to the heart. On this occasion, our Lord was at Philippi, and He asked the disciples a very important question: ". . . whom do *men* say that I the Son of Man am? And they said, Some say that thou art John the Baptist: some, Elias; and others, Jeremias, or one of the prophets."

Then our Lord asked them a second question (v. 15): "But whom say *ye* that I am?" Peter gave that wonderful and classic answer, "Thou art the Christ, the Son of the living God." How did Peter find out? Was he more intellectual than those who said Jesus was John the Baptist, or Elijah, or Jeremiah? Was he more moral?

No! No! Our Lord gives us the answer in verse 17, " . . . blessed art thou, Simon Barjona: for flesh and blood did not *reveal* this to you but my Father who is in heaven." Christ must be *revealed* to the heart as the *only one* who can meet our spiritual need.

This is exactly what the great apostle said about his coming to Christ (Gal. 1:15, 16): "But when it pleased God, who separated me from my mother's womb, and called me by his grace, to *reveal* his Son in me. . . ."

Christ must be *revealed* by the Word and Spirit. This is the second thing *involved* in "coming to Christ" — *a revela-*

tion of Christ to the heart as the only one suitable to meet that spiritual need.

The third thing involved in "coming to Christ" is that there must be a *commitment* of oneself to Christ *without reservation* as the *only one* who can meet that need.

In Mark 10:17–22, we see this in our Lord's evangelism. Observe him dealing with the rich young ruler. The young man obviously had a reservation, and when Jesus pressed this point, the man turned away. But, Jesus did not lower the standard to accommodate him. The Bible shows that Jesus let him go.

In Matthew 13:45, 46, the same principle is seen in our Lord's parable: "Again, the kingdom of heaven is like unto a merchant man, seeking goodly pearls: Who, when he had found one pearl of great price, went and sold *all* that he had, and bought it." This is the principle — *without reservations*.

Anything less than these three things is to be a stranger to the Christ of the Bible and true Christianity.

To have a clear biblical picture of what is involved in coming to Christ will have a profound effect on our evangelistic methods. And be sure, this understanding will make our *methods* God-centered and God-honoring.

8. IS THERE A DIVINE METHOD?

If there is a divine method, we should expect to find it in the divine manual. Yes, we have a divine manual for evangelism—the Book of Acts. This is what the Book of Acts is all about. It begins with evangelism (Acts 1:8): "But ye shall receive power, after that the Holy Ghost is come upon you: and ye shall be witnesses unto me both in Jerusalem, and in all Judaea, and in Samaria, and unto the uttermost part of the earth." The whole Book of Acts and all of church history is a record of carrying out the mandate of this verse.

In the Book of Acts, the apostolic messages are recorded; here their methods are recorded. Here the purest efforts of evangelism are recorded, and here we can see the dynamic union of a biblical doctrinal foundation joined with warm heavenly zeal. Here we see a few insignificant people who took Jesus seriously about spreading His truth. No money, no church building, no church politics, no political influence, no influential people, no institutions, no facilities, — but they had the God-centered *message* and the God-centered *methods*. They had a *divine command — "Go."* They had the *Word* of the Lord and the *Spirit* of the Lord. They began with a prayer meeting (Acts 1:14), but they didn't pray for 20 years, "Lord make me a witness." He already did that, and if you are a Christian, you need not pray "Lord make me a witness." He has already done that (Acts 1:8; John 20:21: ". . . as my Father hath sent me even so send I you").

The Bible teaches that everyone who is called into the blessing and benefits of the gospel is also called into the defense and proclamation of the gospel. This does not mean, however, that everyone is called into active verbal confrontation with sinners in defense and proclamation of the gospel, just as everyone is not called to be a public preacher or missionary. But, as part of the church, everyone is called to the defense and proclamation of the gospel because evangelism is the mission of the church, and therefore, every church member has some part of the mission of the church. Paul thanks God for the fellowship of the Philippians in the gospel: "For your fellowship in the gospel from the first day unto now" (Phil. 1:5).

1. They had a divine message: the gospel.
2. They had a divine command: Go spread it.
3. They had a divine promise for power: "ye shall receive power."

WHAT ABOUT THEIR METHODS?

Thank God, their *message* and *methods* are both found in the sacred manual of evangelism. Fundamental to their method were these three ingredients:

1. They worshipped Christ: "they worshipped Him" (Matt. 28:17).
2. They prayed: "These all continued with one accord in prayer and supplication, with the women, and Mary the mother of Jesus, and with his brethren" (Acts 1:14).
3. There was a constant appeal to the Holy Scriptures in all their sermons.

The Book of Acts documents two steps in the biblical method.

The First Was "Go," Contact the Unconverted.

They started with one hundred, twenty (Acts 1:15). Then there was the one and only occasion when three thousand were added to the church (Acts 2:41). Acts 2:47 tells us "the Lord added." In Acts 2:47, again, we see the word "added": "Praising God, and having favour with all the people. And the Lord added to the church daily such as should be saved." And in Acts 4:4, the count was five thousand — and they were still in Jerusalem: "Howbeit many of them which heard the word believed; and the number of the men was about five thousand."

It was a very difficult field. Jerusalem had plenty of religion. Every house, everyone's aunt, uncle and cousin were Jews. But, they were Jews that needed to be converted: "Neither is there salvation in any other: for there is none other name under heaven given among men, whereby we must be saved" (Acts 4:12).

Now, converting these Jews just could not be done. But they didn't know it could not be done, so they simply obeyed the Lord's "Go ye," and He did the converting, and many were "added": "Praising God, and having favour with all the people. And the Lord added to the church daily such as should be saved" (Acts 2:47).

This kind of result demands our consideration of their methods.

The Second Was "Preaching and Teaching" to the Unconverted.

At this point I am not making any effort to distinguish between preaching and teaching. But, whatever that difference is, one thing is certain: all biblical preaching has much sound teaching in it. I suggest you get your Bible and open it to the Book of Acts. In the very first verse we learn our Lord's method. Acts 1:1: ". . . all that Jesus began to do and *teach*."

We learn the same thing from His example as we find it in the gospel and in His instructions. Matthew 28:19: "Go ye therefore, and *teach* all nations. . ."; and Matthew 28:20:

"*teaching* them. . . ." He did not say "decision" them, but *"teach"* them. "He went round the villages, *teaching*" (Mark 6:6). "And Jesus . . . was moved with compassion toward them, because they were as sheep not having a shepherd" (Mark 6:34). What did He do? Call for decisions? No! No! He began to *teach* them. "And Jesus went about all Galilee *teaching* and preaching" (Matt. 4:23).

See our Lord after the resurrection on the way to Emmaus (Luke 24). What did He do? He opened the Scriptures (Luke 24:25-27). He opened their understanding (Luke 24:16, 31, 45).

He never made a direct appeal to the emotions or the will before He instructed their minds.

This is a lesson many preachers and evangelists need to learn. The direct appeal must be to the mind and the understanding, and then, through the *mind* and the *understanding*, we appeal to the *affections* and the *will*. The gospel is a message that contains information and, therefore, must be communicated by definable words. The gospel contains information and needs explanation and application by word and power. "For our gospel came not unto you in word only, but also in power, and in the Holy Ghost, and in much assurance. . ." (I Thess. 1:5).

Now, coming back to the sacred manual for evangelism, we find the apostles used the same method:

> Acts 5:21: ". . . they entered into the temple early in the morning, and *taught*."

> Acts 5:25: We find them standing in the temple evangelizing. What was their method? *"Teaching* the people."

> Acts 5:28: How were they evangelizing Jerusalem? ". . . ye have filled Jerusalem with your *teaching*."

> Acts 11:26: Paul and Barnabas were evangelizing Antioch for a whole year. What was their method? "For a

whole year at Antioch Paul and Barnabas *taught* much people." (Please note: There is not one mention of decisioning people here or in the whole Book of Acts.)

Acts 14:21: At Derbe they used the same method— preaching and teaching—make disciples. (You make disciples by teaching them.)

Acts 15:35: Again, they used the same method— *teaching* and preaching.

Acts 18:11: Paul labored at Corinth for one year and six months evangelizing. How? "And he continued there a year and six months *teaching* the Word of God among them."

Acts 8: We have an example of personal evangelism from the sacred manual of evangelism. Philip was evangelizing the Ethiopian treasurer. Please note his method and the total absence of "decisionism." Yes, there was a decision, but not "decisionism." Philip *explained* the Scriptures! That was the method our Lord used, Peter used, Paul used — *teaching,* instructing the mind — then came the decision to confess by baptism what he had embraced from the heart. His mind was instructed, his affections were moved toward Christ, and the will responded to the truth that came to his mind and heart.

The great apostle told young Timothy to do the work of an evangelist (II Tim. 4:5). How did he tell him to do it? Not by going around getting men to decide they know not what. Yes, there is a decision involved. But, Paul told him the God-centered method (II Tim. 2:2): "And the things that thou hast heard of me among many witnesses, the same commit thou to faithful men, who shall be able to *teach* others also."

Timothy knew how he himself had come to salvation: "And that from a child thou hast known the holy scriptures, which are able to make thee wise unto salvation through faith which is in Christ Jesus'' (II Tim. 3:15). He was taught the Holy Scriptures.

When will someone open the sacred manual of evangelism and use the God-centered method as we find it in Holy Scriptures? The gospel is a message that must be learned before it can be embraced and before it can be lived or applied. I pray that Christians would rebel against man-centered methods of evangelism and return to the God-centered methods clearly outlined in the New Testament. We learn our methods from the Great Commission (Matt. 28:19): "Go ye therefore and *teach* all nations. . . ." The word *teach* in our King James version is also rendered more accurately *make disciples,* which is more of a reference to the product than the method of producing. However, the method of *producing* disciples is *teaching.*

My continued appeal is to our Lord's method and the apostolic method as we find it in the Gospels and the Book of Acts. It would be wonderful if all who are engaged in evangelism would just open their Bibles to Acts and study it with some important questions in mind as to its content.

1. What was the apostles' *message*? (Study their sermons and their conversations with the unconverted for the answer.)
2. What was their *method* in dealing with the unconverted?

Open your Bible, and if you are just half-honest with the Scriptures, you will find that their efforts consisted in presenting Jesus Christ to sinful men, in order that through the power of the Holy Spirit, sinners may be reconciled to God through Christ and come to put their trust in God, through Him, to receive Christ as their Savior from sin and its consequences, and to serve Him in the fellowship of His church. All their methods were consistent with their goal, and therefore, both their *message* and *method* were *God-*

centered, God-honoring, and God-owned.

WHAT WERE THE RESULTS?

Again, I appeal to the sacred manual of evangelism. Looking at the results from the human side, many times the apostles looked like failures. They made people angry; they wound up in jail; they were threatened, persecuted, and killed; but *they did not change their message or their method.*

After Peter's sermon (Acts 3:12–26) he was arrested and threatened. After Stephen's sermon (Acts 7), Stephen was arrested and finally stoned to death. Our Lord's chief evangelist, Paul, was beaten and jailed and finally ended his evangelistic career by having his noble head severed from his tired shoulders by the shining sword of Nero (II Tim. 4). But, *they did not change their message or their method.* They did not have a committee, or congress, or symposium on evangelism to come up with some new carnal methods. They did not say, "This is not working; we better have more music, or put on a little more 'gospel entertainment.' " No! No! They continued to use the same method—*teaching and preaching* the biblical message.

The first question with the early followers of Christ was not, Does it *work?* or, How many did you *baptize?* but, *Is it true, is it biblical?* They were committed to the truth and left the results to God. And they did not abandon the church and say, "Well, the church is not doing the job," and, therefore, go out and form a "St. Peter's, Inc. for Christ," or, a "St. Paul Crusade for Christ," because Christ founded a church—"the Lord added to the *church.*"

After one of the greatest evangelistic sermons ever preached, by the greatest evangelist that ever lived, the results are recorded like this: some *mocked;* some said, "we will hear you again"—others *believed;* and there was no follow-up program for those who believed. They worshipped God and witnessed for God. *Why no follow-up program?* Because in God-centered evangelism, God does something inwardly to sinners. It is not so much what the sinner does, but what God does. What the sinner does is the result of what God does. And when God does what only God can do, the sinner *always* does what he must do — *repent* toward God, *believe* the gospel and follow Christ. Follow-up is not necessary—the sinner willingly becomes a follower. Then, and then alone, God adds to the church: "The Lord added to the church" (Acts 2:47). Note well, "added *to the church,*" not some man-made, man-centered organization.

When I say follow-up is not necessary, I do not mean that we are not meant to *teach* and *encourage* them to grow in grace and knowledge of our Lord and Savior, but what I mean is cajoling and pampering and begging them to do what everyone who is born again will want to do and will do without calling them every week to remind them and coerce them to worship and serve the Lord in His church.

In the New Testament evangelism, there was preaching, teaching, reasoning, explaining, persuading and pleading. All of this was before a decision. Man-centered evangelism is chiefly concerned with "decisioning," and in many cases, the person does not know what is involved in the decision, or exactly what he is deciding, or why he is making the decision. "For Christ sent me not to baptize, but to *preach* . . . . it pleased God by the foolishness of *preaching* to save them that believe. . . . we *preach* Christ crucified. . ." (I Cor. 1:17, 21, 23).

9. SUMMARY AND COMPARISON

In order to sum up the differences that we have considered thus far between God-centered and man-centered evangelism, the following is a comparison in four vital areas of biblical truth as it relates to evangelism.

1. The difference in the view of the character of God as we deal with sinners — particularly in our point of contact with the unconverted.
2. The difference in the views of man as to his condition before God.
3. The difference in the views of the person and work of Christ as it relates to evangelism.
4. The difference in the views of the sinner's response to Christ.

THE VIEW OF THE CHARACTER OF GOD

Man-centered evangelism at the point of contact with non-Christians usually begins with the love of God—"God loves you"—not with "God created you," and therefore has authority over you as your Maker and Judge.

God-centered evangelism follows the example of the great New Testament preacher and evangelist, the apostle Paul, with the unconverted pagans at Athens. He did not begin with "God loves you" but "God *made* you" (creation). Therefore God has authority over you and your destiny (cf. Acts 17:22–31). This is a biblical example of the God-centered approach to the unconverted. I am not striving for the wording, but the necessity of seeing a breach in the Creator-creature relationship before a Redeemer relationship will make sense. Jesus came to reconcile us to God; therefore, it is necessary to see the need of reconciliation.

"God loves you." It is true that the love of God for sinners sent Christ to the cross, but it is equally true that His *justice* sent Christ to the cross. The base of the cross is God satisfying divine justice so that sinners will have an honorable pardon, not a sentimental pardon.

A prophetic passage that probably best describes the work of the cross is Isaiah 42:21: ". . . he will magnify the law, and make it honorable. . . ." At the cross Christ magnified the law and satisfied divine justice.

Therefore, it is important to see the complete picture of the cross. The base of the cross is eternal justice—the spirit of the cross is eternal love.

We have the same principle illustrated in our Lord's example. See Him evangelize the woman at the well. After a gentle and tactful approach about water and thirst (her real problem was not water and thirst, but adultery), He immediately tells her to call her husband. Well, what was He doing? The context clearly shows that He was bringing her to the Creator's mandate that says, "Thou shalt not commit adultery"—again, the principle of sinners seeing the breach in the Creator-creature relationship.

See Him again, using the same principle with the rich young ruler (Mark 10). In this case the young man's problem was not adultery like the woman at the well. His problem was with the Creator's mandate that says, "Thou shalt have no other gods before me." Money was his god. Again, see that the breach in the Creator-creature relationship is essential before reconciliation by the Redeemer makes sense.

". . . God, who hath reconciled us to himself by Jesus Christ, and hath given us the ministry of reconciliation . . . hath committed unto us the word of reconciliation. Now then we are ambassadors for Christ, as though God did beseech you by us: we pray you in Christ's stead, be ye reconciled to God'' (II Cor. 5:18–20). From this passage it is easy to see the biblical principle that man must see the breach between the Creator and the creature before he will desire reconciliation.

Man-centered evangelism operates with disharmony in the Trinity with respect to the accomplishment and application of God's salvation. Man-centered evangelism says God the Father planned the salvation of every individual ever born, and that Christ died savingly for every individual without exception, but the Holy Spirit applies that salvation only to those who believe, and since all do not believe, God's plan did not work, and Christ's person and work did not accomplish all that He intended. Thus, we have a frustrated and defeated God.

God-centered evangelism operates on the basis that the Trinity works together in perfect harmony; that is, what the Father planned in respect to salvation, the Son purchased on the cross, and the Holy Spirit applies. Therefore, in God-centered evangelism, we do not have a frustrated God, a defeated God, a disappointed Christ, or an impotent Spirit. Every sheep will hear His voice and come to the fold of the great Shepherd. All this is theologically summed up in that golden chain of theology found in Romans 8:29–30: ''For whom he did foreknow [forelove], he also did predestinate to be conformed to the image of his Son, that he might be the first born among many brethren. Moreover whom he did predestinate, them he also called: and whom he called, them he also justified: and whom he justified, them he also glorified.'' It is clearly seen that this honors God, glorifies God and makes all saints lay the crown for their salvation at the feet of God. It is not like man-centered evangelism, which puts the crown for their salvation on their decision.

Man-centered evangelism immediately holds out to sinners a God who is a friend who will help them and solve their problems and deliver them from all of life's casualties.

God-centered evangelism emphasizes that God is our Creator, King, and Ruler of the universe and therefore has *power to save and power to damn.* Without the redeeming merits of Christ, men are at enmity with God and His just wrath hangs over their heads. Only through Christ and His work on the cross are we adopted sons and reconciled friends. The fact that Christ came to reconcile us to God clearly indicates the necessity of reconciliation, and certainly friends do not need to be reconciled.

VIEWS OF MAN AS TO HIS
CONDITION BEFORE GOD

Man-centered evangelism views man as fallen, yet with the ability to come to God and a will that is totally free to choose spiritual good.

God-centered evangelism views man as spiritually deaf, spiritually blind, and spiritually dead, and his will is only free to act according to his nature. And since he is born with a sinful nature (Ps. 51:5: "Behold, I was shapen in iniquity; and in sin did my mother conceive me."), he is only free to act according to his nature. It is because he does not have the will to come to God, or the ability to come, that his great need is *life*, not just help. He needs power that is sufficient to change his mind, affections and will, that is, *almighty power.*

Let us examine this difference from the Holy Scriptures. Apart from a work of the Spirit, will any man choose God? The answer is found in one of the most pessimistic verses in the Bible, that is, John 5:40. Jesus said, "And ye *will not* come unto me, that ye might have life." *"Will not come"*—and until God powerfully does something to man's "willer," he will not *will* to come. Therefore, God-centered evangelism tells sinners to call upon God to do something for them that they cannot do for themselves. Man-centered evangelism tries to get sinners to do something with Jesus. God-centered evangelism tells the sinner that since God must do something, therefore, one needs to call upon God. This posture is seen in such passages as Luke 5:12. Here is a poor leper who is hopeless and helpless. His only hope was in what Jesus could do, not in his decision to do something with Jesus. Therefore, he fell on his face, and the Bible says he besought Jesus to do something: ". . . Lord, if thou wilt, thou canst make me clean" (Luke 5:12). His hope was in the power, the will, and the mercy of Christ. We have the same principle in the posture of blind Bartimaeus: "Jesus, thou son of David, have mercy on me" (Mark 10:47), or, with the publican in Luke 18:13 ". . . God be merciful to me. . . ." The point I am emphasizing is *bowing* to Christ, not trying to get sinners to strike a bargain with Christ.

Man-centered evangelism leaves sinners with the idea that their hope is in their decision. The language goes something like this. "You do this," or "You do that," or "You do the other thing," and God will save you!

The Bible is clear on this point as to the spiritual condition of sinners. It teaches that sinners:

1. Cannot *understand.* I Corinthians 2:14: "But the natural man receiveth not the things of the Spirit of God: for they are foolishness unto him: neither can he know them, because they are spiritually discerned."

2. Cannot *hear.* John 8:43: "Why do ye not understand my speech? even because ye cannot *hear* my word."

3. Cannot *see.* John 3:3: "Jesus answered and said unto him, Verily, verily, I say unto thee, Except a man be born again, he cannot *see* the kingdom of God."

4. Cannot *come.* John 6:44: "No man can *come* to me, except the Father which hath sent me draw him: and I will raise him up at the last day."

5. Cannot be *subject to the law of God.* Romans 8:7:
"Because the carnal mind is enmity against God:
for it is *not subject to the law of God, neither indeed
can be."*

Man-centered evangelism deals with man as though he
has ability to choose spiritual good, is seeking truth, and
needs only the information of the gospel, that is, love, help
and friendship.

God-centered evangelism also believes man needs love,
help and friendship, but according to the above five descriptions of every man born of woman, he needs his understanding, his ears and his eyes opened to receive the information.
He needs the will and ability to come to Christ. He needs
life.

God-centered evangelism therefore believes that man
needs to be changed by power divine. He needs a new
nature. His need is not only to be delivered from the *consequences* of sin, but from a sinful nature, from the power of
sin and its consequences.

To sum it up: God-centered evangelism believes all men
are fallen and will not come to God by their own power or
will, because they are deaf, blind, dead and have no power
for spiritual good. Their minds are at enmity with God, and
left to themselves, they will not seek God. Men need new
natures. We call this *regeneration.* Regeneration is the work
of God alone, and this great work always produces conversion, which is repentance toward God and faith toward our
Lord Jesus Christ. Regeneration is a big theological word
that views salvation from God's side—it is the instantaneous impartation of *life.* Paul calls it *new creation.* One
may, or may not, be conscious of the exact moment when it
takes place in them. Conversion, on the other hand, is viewing salvation from the human side. Repenting is something
man does. Believing is something man does. Both are a
result of what God does. This order is important if you are

ever to understand the difference between God-centered and man-centered evangelism.

Joshiah Conder expressed the order in a hymn:

'Tis not that I did choose thee, For, Lord that could
   not be;
  This heart would still refuse thee, Hadst thou not
    chosen me.
Thou from the sin that stained me hast cleansed and set
   me free;
  Of old thou hast ordained me, that I should live to thee.
'Twas sov'reign mercy called me and taught my op'ning
   mind;
  The world had else enthralled me, to heav'nly glories
    blind.
My heart owns none before thee, for thy rich grace I
   thirst;
  This knowing, if I love thee, Thou must have loved me
    first.

Another hymn that has the cause and the means of salvation in the proper order is:

I sought the Lord, and afterward I knew
  He moved my soul to seek him, seeking me;
It was not I that found, O Saviour true,
  No, I was found of thee.

Thou didst reach forth thy hand and mine enfold;
  I walked and sank not on the storm-vexed sea,
'Twas not so much that I on thee took hold,
  As thou, dear Lord, on me.

I find, I walk, I love, but O the whole
  Of love is but my answer, Lord to thee.
For thou wert long before-hand with my soul
  Always thou lovedst me.

The apostle John put it this way: "We love him *because*

He *first* loved us."

Man-centered evangelism does not have a correct view of the relationship between the cause of conversion and the means God employs in conversion.

VIEWS OF THE PERSON AND WORK OF CHRIST AS IT RELATES TO EVANGELISM

The third area where God-centered and man-centered evangelism differ vastly is in respect to the person and work of Christ.

Man-centered evangelism puts the emphasis on Christ's saviorhood: that He is a Savior from our selfishness, our mistakes—a Savior from life's casualties, and a Savior from the consequences of sin. Thus Christ came and exists for our benefit.

God-centered evangelism puts the emphasis on Christ as the Savior from sin and its consequences, but more important, from the sinful nature, which is the root cause of every sin. In other words, Christ came not only to *save* us, but by His Spirit, to *change* us. "Therefore, if any man be in Christ, he *is* a new creature [new creation] . . . ." Please note, II Corinthians 5:17 says, *"is a new creature,"* not "likely will become a new creature." Christ not only does things *for* us, but He does something *in* us.

Reader, don't be deceived with this generation of poor, lost church members who have not been changed within by the power of Christ's Spirit. Be sure of this: if the blood of Christ covers your record in heaven (justification), the Spirit of Christ does something in your heart on earth (sanctification begun). To put it theologically, justification and sanctification are graces inseparably joined together in the application of God's salvation. This is made crystal clear in the blessings of the new covenant that Christ came to enact by His person and work. The Bible says He is the Mediator of the new covenant. And that covenant has two parts:

One part is that ". . . their sins and iniquities will I remember no more" [justification—something that takes place in heaven by the blood of Christ] (Heb. 8:12).

The other part of the covenant is ". . . I will put my laws into their hearts and in their minds will I write them. . ." [sanctification — something that takes place on earth] (Heb. 8:10; 10:16). Be sure of this—if nothing has taken place on earth in your heart by the Spirit of Christ, there is no reason to believe that anything has taken place in heaven, by the blood of Christ. The Spirit and the blood are inseparably joined together in the application of God's salvation.

God-centered evangelism emphasizes both parts of the new covenant at the outset. Man-centered evangelism emphasizes the first part of the covenant at the outset and makes the second part optional.

To solve this awful error of separating justification and sanctification, man-centered evangelism has invented many strange and erroneous doctrines, under a thousand different names and forms of "second works of grace" teachings, such as the damning doctrine of the divided Christ (taking Christ as your Savior, and then later, making Christ "Lord," or the "victorious life," "abundant life," "higher life," "triumphant life," and "taste of new wine" teachings. They are born because of the error of man-centered evangelism that in practice separates what God has joined in the new covenant, namely, justification and sanctification. This is not an attack on the person or character of some of the godly and able men who teach some form of a second work of grace. However, any second work of grace teaching reveals an improper understanding of the new covenant (Heb. 8:10–12; 10:16, 17), that is, the biblical teaching of the relationship between justification and sanctification or the nature of saving faith.[1] (See Appendix.)

God-centered evangelism does not separate what Christ's blood does in heaven and what His Spirit does on earth. Here lies one of the main differences in the two views in respect to the Person and Work of Christ. Which view honors God? Which one is true to the new covenant?

THE DIFFERENCE IN THE TWO VIEWS IN RESPECT TO THE SINNER'S RESPONSE TO CHRIST

For our gospel came not unto you in word only,
but also in power, and in the Holy Ghost, and in
much assurance; as ye know what manner of men
we were among you for your sake (I Thess. 1:5).

When the gospel comes to sinners in *word* and *power,* it not only summons, draws forth, elicits, and evokes a decision, but also powerfully engages the *mind*, powerfully moves the *affections*, and powerfully changes the *will*. In other words, it powerfully reaches and changes the *whole man*, therefore, the *whole man* responds. God-centered evangelism is aimed at the *whole man* and calls for a response from the *whole man*. There is a very important reason for this. The reason is that true religion cannot be less than:

1. Right *thinking* in relationship to God.
2. Right *feeling* in relationship to God.
3. Right *acting* in relationship to God.

This is the *whole man: mind, affections, will.*

At this point there are two basic errors in man-centered evangelism. First, there are those who aim at the intellect (mind) only. Now, this is the right place to begin, and it is very important to do so; however, it is not the end. Man is

---

[1] I recommend J. C. Ryle's *Holiness;* John Owen, Volume 6; A. W. Pink's *Saving Faith.*

more than *mind,* and the error comes when the sinner's only response is an intellectual response, that is, the sinner, being able to give the right answers to the proper questions. The error lies in the fact that a man can learn religious truth intellectually, just as he can learn history, mathematics, English, geography or philosophy. Children can learn the right answers to good catechism questions, or memorize Scripture passages, and yet never be affected by the truth because it has never reached their affections or wills.

Intellectual understanding can be acquired without the work of the Holy Spirit in the heart. There must be the application of biblical truth to the affections and to the will, and only the Spirit can apply Bible truth efficaciously.

Let me try to illustrate my point. When we build a fire in the fireplace, we must lay the logs in the fireplace. We can lay the logs very carefully, but we need more than logs. A match must be struck to ignite the flame. If there are no logs, there will be no fire, but the logs must be lit or there will be no fire. No logs—no fire. No match—no fire. So with divine truth. We must lay the logs of divine truth to the mind, but without the Spirit coming in power to illuminate the mind, there will be no true conversion. The Spirit must open the understanding, make truth alive and effectual. A good biblical illustration is the case of Lydia's conversion recorded in Acts 16:14, 15. She heard the word, she heeded the word, but between hearing and heeding, God did something; the Bible says, *"The Lord opened her heart."*

The second error of man-centered evangelism in respect to the response is an approach that is aimed at the emotions only. This is usually done with many anecdotes, experiences, deathbed stories, etc., but not true biblical exposition or Christian doctrine. And, of course, in many cases, the response is purely emotional. Oh yes! there was a religious experience. There was a response from the sinner, but, sad to say, many times it proves not to be a saving response or a saving experience. Rather, it is only an emotional experience.

Bishop J. C. Ryle, the great bishop of Liverpool, whom God used to found about 25 churches, had it right when he said, "You can talk about religious experiences all you wish, but, if it does not have doctrinal roots, it is like cut flowers stuck into the ground. They will soon wither and die." How many times have we seen it?

The God-centered approach is to address the whole man with a whole Christ, the Christ of the Bible who is Prophet, Priest and King of His church. The whole Christ must be preached and the whole man must respond.

Another difference in respect to the sinner's response to Christ is that, in man-centered evangelism, the sinner's choice, decision, and response is the basis of his salvation—"I made my decision for Christ and am saved." Or "My decision for Christ changed my life." This is the language of a man-centered response to Christ, and there is some truth in it. But it is only half truth, and when half truth is treated as the whole truth, the result is complete falsehood.

In God-centered evangelism, the sinner's response and decision is because of God's decision, God's power, and God's initiative in saving. The gospel comes to the sinner in *word and power*—not just in word. The language of God-centered evangelism is more like this: "God magnified His grace and power in the salvation of my soul." God saves sinners; therefore, the testimony emphasizes what God did because the Christian knows what he did was only a result of what God did. His decision was not the cause of God doing something for him, but rather, a result of what God did. This difference is not just semantics, but a difference in biblical content, substance, and theology.

When this is understood, there will be no more of this man-centered method of begging sinners to respond to an impotent Savior who is standing idly by, patiently and path-etically waiting for the sinner's response. No! No! But rather, it will be lifting up a powerful Savior who is ready, able and willing to save all that come to God by Him. The sinner must come to this Savior who actually saves, not one who just makes salvation possible.

The preachers and evangelists who hold to this God-centered view will set forth the Christ of the Bible as one who actually saves sinners by purpose and by power: "For the Son of man is come to seek and to save that which was lost" (Luke 19:10). Man-centered evangelism presents a Savior who only makes salvation possible, and its success depends on the sinner's response.

Let me try to illustrate this from a New Testament exam-ple. The case of blind Bartimaeus (Mark 10:46-52). Blind Bartimaeus was sitting helplessly by the side of the road, and when he heard that Jesus was passing by, he did not say volitionally, "Now I am going to make a decision to follow Jesus." No! His only hope was in something that Jesus, and only Jesus, could do. What did he do? He did what every sinner *must* do — he asked Jesus to do something for him that he could not do for himself. Listen to his cry: ". . . he began to cry out, and say, Jesus, thou Son of David, have mercy on me. . . ." This is the posture, that is, the response of a sinner in God-centered evangelism.

Read the sacred manual of evangelism and one of the God-centered principles you will discover is what we see in the case of blind Bartimaeus, that is, the principle of *boxing sinners up to the mercy of God and the power of God.*

Man-centered evangelism contains much truth, such as, that a man must make a decision—he must experience re-pentance toward God and exercise faith toward our Lord Jesus Christ. True, but that is only half of the truth. The other half (often left out all together or so obscured that it is not recognized) is that no man will make this saving response unless God first does what only God can do, that is, the work of *regeneration*. God commands all men to repent (Acts 17:30), and God commands men to believe (I John 3:23)—"And this is his commandment, that we should believe on the name of his Son Jesus Christ. . . ."

What God commands, He supplies. This is why the gospel must come not in Word only, but also in *power*. That power does not reside in the sinner's ability, or in his will to respond, or in the preacher's power to persuade, but in the mighty power of God to quicken (regenerate) poor, dead sinners. And where God does this mighty work, faith and repentance always follow—yes, I said always.

10. WHY DO SOME SINNERS COME TO CHRIST WHILE OTHERS DO NOT?

And the servant of the Lord must not strive; but be gentle unto all men, apt to teach, patient, in meekness instructing those that oppose themselves; if God peradventure will give them repentance to the acknowledging of the truth; and that they may recover themselves out of the snare of the devil, who are taken captive by him at his will.

— II Tim. 2:24–26

This passage is very relevant to our whole subject of evangelism because here we have one of the greatest evangelists who ever lived giving instructions to one who was told to ". . . do the work of an evangelist. . ." (II Tim. 4:5). Surely these two facts demand our careful and sober consideration. If we are serious about being biblical in our evangelism, we cannot ignore these instructions.

There are several things in these few verses that would correct much of the error in man-centered evangelism, not only in the expected responses, but in the message and methods of evangelism. Let us carefully examine this passage, which contains instructions to one who was given an apostolic command to do the work of an evangelist. In this passage (II Tim. 2:24–26), we have some excellent instructions for the evangelist, preacher, and personal worker, and some necessary evangelistic principles if our evangelism is to be God-centered.

STATE OF THE UNCONVERTED

Every preacher should know the condition of the un-converted.

1. He is ignorant of saving truth. This is clearly seen in the words in verse 25, ". . . in meekness *instructing* those. . . ." They need instruction because they are ignorant of spiritual truth.

2. He is a slave to Satan, which is seen in the words in verse 26: ". . . that they may recover themselves out out the *snare of the devil. . . ."*

3. He is a captive of Satan (in Satan's prison house), verse 26: ". . .*taken captive* by him [Satan] at his will."

Who Has the Key — God or the Sinner?

Both man-centered and God-centered evangelism believe that sinners are ignorant of spiritual realities; they are slaves to Satan, and in Satan's prison. The difference is that man-centered evangelism tells the sinner he has the key in his pocket to get out any time he wills to get out. The appeal is to the sinner's will, his decision and his power to do something for himself. This is the opposite of the New Testament principle of boxing up the unconverted to hope in God alone and in God's power.

God-centered evangelism also believes that sinners are ignorant of spiritual realities—that they are slaves to Satan, and in Satan's prison, and worse, that they are on death row. God-centered evangelism does not flatter the sinner or try to give him hope by telling him that he has the key in his pocket to get out at will, because the unconverted are all by nature unwilling and unable.

The God-centered approach is to tell him he is in Satan's prison house, yes, and he is on death row, and that he does not have the key in his pocket to get out! If anyone gets him out, it will have to be God. The sinner's only hope is in

God's mercy and God's power.

This God-centered truth is found in the passage before us in the words, "*If perhaps God.*" The sinner's only hope is in "*God*" (verse 25: "*If perhaps God*" will do something). This truth is not only hopeful to the sinner, but it is very hopeful to the preacher. The preacher's only hope of a saving response is "*if perhaps God*" will do something for the sinner that he cannot do for himself and that no preacher can do for him. Please remember, this was written to a young preacher who was meant to do the work of an *evangelist* (II Tim. 4:5). This fact should give weight to all I am saying on this point. Certainly we should expect fo find some principles for evangelism in these Epistles.

EFFORTS OF THE SERVANT OF GOD

We also have in this passage the *efforts* that this young preacher was to exercise.

1. Teach and instruct (v. 24: ". . . apt to teach . . ."; v. 25: ". . . in meekness instructing. . .").
2. Rescue them, if possible, from Satan (v. 26: ". . . that they may recover themselves out of the snare of the devil. . .").
3. Set before them the claims of God as their only hope, not just tell deathbed stories, seeking a psychological response.

MANNER AND METHOD EMPLOYED BY THE SERVANT OF GOD

The passage also has the instructions as to the *manner and method* to be employed. "*The servant of the Lord. . .*" (v. 24):

1. Must not strive (or be quarrelsome).
2. Must be *gentle* (be kind to all).
3. Must be *able to teach*.
4. Must be *patient* (when wronged).

5. Must instruct in *meekness* (with gentleness).

Think how much more biblical and God-centered evangelism would be if all the zealous preachers and evangelists would have heeded these clear instructions found in this passage.

What I am trying to show is that the Bible teaches that evangelism is a work of *divine grace, divine power, divine sovereignty*. Therefore, if evangelism is to be true, biblical evangelism, it must be *God-centered* and aim at a God-centered response from the sinner.

11. THE NATURE OF THE RESPONSE

Another difference of the two views in respect to the sinner's response is the implication of the response. The response in God-centered evangelism implies:

1. Loving submission to Christ's lordship at the outset, not later at a second work of grace or a second act of consecration: "And why call ye me Lord, Lord, and do not the things which I say?" (Luke 6:46).

2. Willing obedience: "if ye love me keep my commandments. . . . Jesus answered and said . . . if a man loves me he will keep my words. . . . He that loveth me not keepeth not my sayings" (John 14:15, 24). Obedience is not something that is presented to sinners later on as an option.

3. Ownership: ". . . ye are not your own . . . for ye are bought with a price. . ." (I Cor. 6:19, 20); "they forsook all and followed him. . . . And he left all, rose up, and followed him" (Luke 5:11, 28).

4. Joyful service: ". . . Lord, what wilt thou have me to do?" (Acts 9:6—the disposition of a new convert). We see this also in I Thessalonians 1:9: "For they themselves shew of us what manner of entering in we had unto you, and how ye turned to God from idols to serve the living and true God." These converts did three things: (1) turned to God (faith), (2) turned from idols (repentance), (3) served the living and true God.

This is the response of the sinner in God-centered evangelism.

Man-centered evangelism usually emphasizes the benefits and blessings of coming to Christ, and later begins to emphasize discipleship as something that is optional. Many times invitations are like funnels: they are big and wide at the beginning in order to get sinners in; they then must squeeze sinners through a narrow passage. The squeezing process often reveals the lack of real Christian experience at the beginning.

In the New Testament, converts were called Christians because they were disciples: ". . .the disciples were called Christians . . ." (Acts 11:26). They were disciples first. Our Lord put the little end of the funnel first: "Enter ye in at the strait gate: for wide is the gate, and broad is the way, that leadeth to destruction, and many there be which go in thereat: Because strait is the gate, and narrow is the way, which leadeth unto life, and few there be that find it" (Matt. 7:13, 14). You will note the narrow gate is at the beginning of the way, not some later option.

Our Lord was honest in inviting men at the outset. Again hear Him inviting sinners to follow Him: "And he said unto them all, If any man will come after me, let him deny himself, and take up his cross daily, and follow me" (Luke 9:23). In Luke 14:25-33, He is speaking to "great multitudes." He tells them to count the cost in the invitation (vv. 26, 27): "If any man come to me, and hate not his father, and mother, and wife, and children, and brethren, and sisters, yea, and his own life also, he cannot be my disciple. And whosoever doth not bear his cross, and come after me, cannot be my disciple." Then to underscore the cost, He uses two illustrations. In His first illustration (vv. 28-30) he speaks of a man who started to build a tower but could not finish it. Why? Because he did not first count the cost.

Our Lord's second illustration is found in verses 31 and

32. He illustrates His point by a king going to war who does not anticipate the strength of his enemy. Our Lord then makes the application of His illustrations (v. 33): "So likewise, whosoever he be of you that forsaketh not all that he hath, he cannot be my disciple." His invitation was honest at the beginning about the cost.

Let me show you further just how honest He was in respect to His invitation. In Luke 9:57 we have a man who said to Jesus, "Lord, I will follow thee whithersoever thou goest." Now, what would most preachers or evangelists do in such a case? They would immediately add him to their statistics and say, "Man, I have been looking for you — come along." And, in two weeks, he would have been teaching a Sunday school class. But Jesus was honest at the invitation, and please note what He said (v. 58): "And Jesus said unto him, Foxes have holes, and birds of the air have nests; but the Son of man hath not where to lay his head." Not a very good way to build up your statistics, but it was honest.

The Christian life is not a "gospel hayride." It is hard to be a real Christian, and it costs something to be a Christian. When Jesus was telling men to count the cost, He was not talking about the price of redemption—that is infinite. We are not redeemed with ". . . corruptible things, as silver and gold . . . But with the precious blood of Christ. . ." (I Peter 1:18, 19). It costs to be a Christian—not to become a Christian.

Man-centered evangelism tends to hold out the joys and blessings and the hope of heaven, but does not face the other half, that is, of what it costs to follow Christ. In this we have an example of the danger of spreading half-truths for the whole truth. It becomes the worst kind of perversion.

Just think of some of the pain that would be spared in the church if men had been as honest as our Lord was at the beginning. The quantity may not be as great, but the quality would be better and much more fruitful.

Many of the responses in man-centered evangelism are faulty because the invitation did not contain the whole truth at the outset. *There is a relationship between the invitation given and the response expected,* or to put it another way, *there is a relationship between the seeds sown and the harvest reaped.*

12. ASSURANCE OF GRACE
AND SALVATION

*These things have I written unto you that believe
on the name of the Son of God; that ye may know
that ye have eternal life, and that ye may believe
on the name of the Son of God.*

— I John 5:13

*Wherefore the rather, brethren, give diligence to
make your calling and election sure: for if ye do
these things ye shall never fall.*

— II Peter 1:10

The doctrine of assurance is vitally related to evangelism,
but before we consider assurance and evangelism, let us
look at the importance of the biblical doctrine of assurance.

It is important to have a clear understanding of the biblical teaching of assurance for all spiritual evangelistic counseling. It is just here where many poor souls are mislead and
often deceived about their salvation. Here is where the
pastor or personal worker functions as a spiritual surgeon.

It is also important because a well-grounded assurance is
related to joy, comfort, and Christian service. How can one
have the *joy* of salvation if he is not sure he is in possession
of salvation? How can one have the *comfort* of salvation if
he does not have the assurance of salvation?

Assurance is a God-given conviction of our standing in
grace stamped on the mind and heart by the Spirit of God
supernaturally. It is a conscious and experimental discern-

ing of a saving relationship with God.

William Cunningham, a respected theologian, said, "We believe that the prevailing practical disregard of the privileges and duty of having assurance is, to no inconsiderable extent, the cause and effect of the low state of vital religion among us."

James Denny, the author of *The Death of Christ,* a great classic on the atonement, said, "The acid test of any version of Christianity is its attitude toward assurance. Some regard it as a presumption; some regard it as a duty; the New Testament proclaims it as a fact."

Thomas Goodwin said, "Assurance is the 'White Stone' (Rev. 22:17) which none knows but he that receives it."

What does the Bible teach about assurance?

First, the Bible teaches that there is a false assurance in which unconverted men sometimes indulge, in which they are deceived, and in which they will finally be discovered. It is possible to place one's hope on insufficient grounds: "The hypocrite's hope shall perish" (Job 8:13). Moreover, "The heart is deceitful. . ." (Jer. 17:9), and ". . . if a man think himself to be something, when he is nothing, he deceiveth himself" (Gal. 6:3). Men are easily deceived in religious matters. The Pharisees were sure they were *"right with God"* and sought to evangelize others: "Woe unto you, scribes and Pharisees, hypocrites! for ye compass sea and land to make one proselyte [convert], and when he is made, ye make him twofold more the child of hell than yourselves" (Matt. 23:15).

It is because of the possibility of religious self-deception that we have the many warnings in the New Testament about the spurious believers. The two houses in Matthew 7 both looked sound and true, but when the storm of God's judgment came, it was manifest that one was real (built upon the rock); the other was not real (built upon the sand). This is one of our Lord's warnings about religious deception. The ten virgins in Matthew 25 all had the lamp of profession and assurance, but five were self-deceived and thought they had assurance saying, "Lord, Lord"; Jesus had to say, ". . . verily I say unto you, I know you not." He said the same thing in His great sermon to those who had much assurance. Hear them express their assurance: "Lord, Lord, have we not prophesied in thy name and in thy name have cast out devils? and in thy name done many wonderful works?" They had much assurance, but our Lord said to them, "I never knew you: depart from me, ye that work iniquity." The Bible teaches that there is a false assurance and gives many warnings against it.

Second, the Bible teaches that there is a true assurance in which believers are not deceived, but rather confirmed, and in which they will not be confounded. This assurance rests upon God's infallible Word: the graces of which the Word speaks in the believer's heart and the testimony of the Spirit which enables the believer to confirm the one by the other. "The Spirit Himself beareth witness with our spirit, that we are the children of God" (Rom. 8:16). "We know that we have passed from death unto life. . ." (I John 3:14).

Since there is a false assurance and a true assurance, a logical question is, What is the difference? Charles Hodge, one of the great theologians of Princeton Seminary, answered this question in the following manner:

A. *True assurance*—begets unfeigned humility.
   False assurance—begets spiritual pride.

B. *True assurance*—leads to increased diligence in practice of holiness.
   False assurance—leads to sloth and self-indulgence (Ps. 51:12, 13, 19).

C. *True assurance*—leads to candid self-examination and a desire to be searched and corrected by God. ("Search me, O God, and know my heart: try me and know my thoughts: And see if there be any wicked way in me, and lead me in the way ever-lasting" Ps. 139:23, 24).

False assurance—leads to a disposition to be satisfied with appearance and avoid accurate investigation.

D. *True assurance*—leads to constant aspiration after more intimate fellowship with God, which is not true of false assurance. ("Beloved, now are we the sons of God, and it doth not yet appear what we shall be: but we know that, when he shall appear, we shall be like him; for we shall see him as he is. And every man that hath this hope in him purifieth himself, even as he is pure"—I John 3:2, 3).

It is *not* the strength of one's convictions which proves the validity of his assurance, but the character of one's convictions.

Third, the Bible teaches that a true believer may lack assurance. The man in Mark 9:24 cried, "I believe; help thou mine unbelief." When he said, *"I believe"* he was *safe*, but when he said, *"help thou mine unbelief"* it showed that he was *not sure*.

It is of great importance to be clear about the distinction between faith and assurance. It explains things which an inquirer in religion sometimes finds hard to understand. Faith, let us remember, is the root, and assurance is the flower. Doubtless you can never have the flower without the root; but you can have the root without the flower.

Faith is that poor trembling woman, who came behind our Lord in the crowd and touched the hem of His garment.

Assurance is Stephen, standing calmly in the midst of his murderers, saying, "I see the heavens opened and the Son of man standing on the right hand of God."

Faith is the penitent thief crying, "Lord, remember me."

Assurance is Job sitting in the dust, covered with sores, saying, "I know that my Redeemer liveth."

Faith is Peter's drowning cry as he began to sink, "Lord, save me."

Assurance is, later, that same Peter, declaring before the council, "There is none other name given under heaven whereby we can be saved, we cannot but speak the things we have seen and heard."

Faith is Saul praying in the house of Judas at Damascus —sorrowful, blind, and alone.

Assurance is that same aged Paul, now a prisoner, calmly looking into the grave saying, "I know whom I have believed," and, "There is a crown laid up for me."

Faith is life. How great the blessing! Who can tell the great gulf between life and death? Yet life may be weak, sickly, unhealthy, painful, trying, worn, burdensome, joyless, to the last.

Assurance is more than life. It is health, strength, power, vigor, energy, comfort, and joy.

Faith is heaven by and by.

Assurance is heaven on earth.

To know the difference between faith and assurance is important in counseling sinners, seekers, and Christians.

Fourth, the Bible teaches that believers should seek to attain a well-grounded assurance.

> Wherefore the rather, brethren, give diligence to make your calling and election sure: for if ye do these things ye shall never fall (II Peter 1:10).

> And we desire that everyone of you do shew the same diligence to the full assurance of hope unto the end (Heb. 6:11).

He that has such a hope can sing, even in prison, as Paul and Silas did.

Fifth, the Bible teaches that a true believer's assurance may be shaken, diminished, and intermitted because of negligence, sin, temptation, or trial. David, in Psalm 51:12

is crying for assurance to be restored: "Restore unto me the joy of thy salvation; and uphold me with thy free spirit." Hear him cry, "Lord, why castest thou off my soul? why hidest thy face from me? (Ps. 88:14). True believers may forfeit their assurance, and yet they are never entirely destitute of that seed of God, and therefore will not be left to sink into utter despair; and their assurance may, by the operation of the Spirit, be in due time revived.

Sixth, the Bible teaches that assurance, instead of encouraging believers to indulge in sin, excites them to the pursuit of holiness. True biblical assurance cannot be attained or preserved without close walking with God in all his commandments and ordinances blameless. "Beloved, now are we the sons of God, and it doth not yet appear what we shall be: but we know that, when he shall appear, we shall be like him; for we shall see him as he is. And every man that hath this hope in him purifieth himself, even as he is pure" (I John 3:2, 3).

Before I make any effort to set out the difference that exists between the God-centered and the man-centered approach in respect to assurance, I want to point out that the ground of salvation and the ground of assurance are two different things. I will do this by asking two questions and will show that the two questions have two different answers.

The first and the most important question anyone can ever seriously ask is *What must I do to be saved?* There is only one biblical answer to this question: "Believe on the Lord Jesus Christ and thou shalt be saved. . . ." "My hope is built on nothing less than Jesus' blood and righteousness." "Nothing in my hand I bring, simply to thy cross I cling."

The second question is, *How do I know that I have believed to the saving of my soul, that is, How do I know that my faith is saving faith?* This has to do with assurance, and there are three answers to this question. To state it another

120

way, there are three grounds of assurance, or three elements of assurance. When speaking about the grounds of assurance be very clear we are speaking of the ways a believer comes to true assurance, *not the ground on which his salvation rests.*

The *first* ground of assurance is the promises of God made alive or real by the Spirit of God. It is not just the promises of God alone. There must be the work of the Spirit —the Word and the Spirit. The Spirit must apply the Word by opening the sinner's understanding. The sinner has two problems. He needs sight because he is spiritually blind, and he needs light. The Bible is the light, "a lamp unto our feet." But light does not help blind people to see. They also need sight. For this reason I emphasize that the first ground of assurance is not only the promises of God, but the promises of God made real or alive by the Spirit of God.

This may be called direct assurance, and this aspect of assurance is of the essence of faith because the principal acts of saving faith consist of accepting, receiving, and resting upon Christ alone for justification, sanctification and eternal life, and it is impossible for one to rest upon Christ for salvation without believing or trusting that he shall be saved by Him. Whoever rests upon a person for doing a certain thing in his favor must have a persuasion or assurance that he will do that thing for him. Thus, this aspect of assurance is so essential to faith that without it, there can be no faith, human or divine. To believe a report is to be persuaded or assured of the truth of the report; to believe a promise is to be persuaded or assured that the promiser will do as he has said. In like manner, to believe in Christ for salvation is to be persuaded or assured that we shall be saved through the grace of our Lord Jesus Christ. Therefore, because of the nature of saving faith, this aspect of assurance is of the essence of faith. This direct element of assurance is the exercise of faith in Christ. It is an indispensable duty which can never be superseded by any amount of evidences.

This direct exercise of faith in Christ is the unfailing source of relief and comfort in the Christian's darkest doubts. For in some of the dark and defeated hours, the Christian will find nothing to assure him by looking inward or by looking for external evidences. We must look to Christ alone, the Son of righteousness, shining still, unchanged and unchangeable—shining in all His glory behind the clouds which may cast a dark and doubtful shadow on our souls.

Again, I want to emphasize, this is not just a promise intellectually grasped or memorized; it requires also the illumination of the Spirit. There is no other cause that can make the promises of salvation effectual but the Spirit of God.

The *second* ground of assurance is the witness of the Spirit.

> The Spirit himself beareth witness with our spirit, that we are the children of God (Rom. 8:16).

> He that believeth on the Son of God hath the *witness* in himself. . . (I John 5:10).

Here we have (1) the Christian described ("He that believeth on the Son of God . . .") and (2) internal satisfaction (assurance) experienced (". . . hath the witness in himself. . . ").

There are differences among the best of theologians and preachers in regard to the manner in which the Spirit gives this testimony; however, there is no disagreement that the witness of the Spirit is one of the grounds of assurance. The greater part of respected divines agree that the Spirit witnesses by means of His operations or the effect produced by Him in the hearts of believers. They reject the idea of an *immediate* testimony or some revelation apart from the Scriptures, and hold that the work of the Spirit is the testimony which He gives, assuring believers of their adoption, and consequent safety.

By the witness of the Spirit, I understand what the great evangelist and preacher, Jonathan Edwards, expounds. Edwards speaks very strongly against the opinion that the Spirit witnesses by way of immediate suggestion or revelation, and he declares that many mischiefs have arisen from this false and delusive notion.

What has misled many in their notion of that influence of the Spirit of God we are speaking of, is the word *witness*, its being called the witness of the Spirit. Hence they have taken it, not to be any effect or work of the Spirit upon the heart, giving evidence from whence men may argue that they are the children of God; but an inward immediate suggestion as though God inwardly spoke to the man, and testified to him, and told him that he was His child, by a kind of secret voice, or impression: not observing the manner in which the word witness or testimony is often used in the New Testament; where such terms often signify, not only a mere declaring and asserting a thing to be true, but holding forth evidence from whence a thing may be argued and proved to be true. Thus (Heb. 2:4), God is said to bear witness, with signs and wonders, and divers miracles and gifts of the Holy Ghost. Now these miracles, here spoken of, are called God's witness, not because they are of the nature of assertions, but evidences and proofs. So also Acts 14:3; John 5:36; 10:25. So the water and the blood are said to bear witness (I John 5:8), not that they spake or asserted anything, but they were proofs and evidences. Indeed the apostle, when in that (Rom. 8:16), he speaks of the Spirit bearing witness with our spirit that we are the children of God, does sufficiently explain himself, if his words were but attended to. What is here expressed is connected with the two preceding verses, as resulting from what the apostle had there said, as every reader may see. The three verses together are thus: "For as many as are led by the Spirit of God, they are the sons of God; for ye have not received the Spirit of bondage again to fear; but ye have received the Spirit of adoption, whereby we cry, Abba, Father: the Spirit Himself beareth witness with our spirit that we are the children of God." Here what the apostle says, if we take it together, plainly shows that what he has respect to, when he speaks of the Spirit's giving us witness or evidence that we are God's children, is his dwelling in us, and leading us, as a spirit of adoption, or spirit of a child, disposing us to behave towards God as to a Father.[1]

This witness of the Spirit to the sonship of believers must never be divorced from the other activities of the Spirit in the sanctification of believers. The Spirit opens their minds to understand the Scriptures. The Spirit unveils to them more and more of the glory of Christ. The Spirit sheds abroad in their hearts the love of God. He stirs up other holy affections and adorns them with the fruits of the Spirit.

The *third* ground of assurance is Christian character and conduct, or assurance by evidence of regeneration, or assurance by the marks of grace. We could call this *First John* assurance, for one could not read this Epistle without seeing that Christian character and conduct have something to do with assurance.

John is writing to strengthen assurance. He tells us that his purpose for writing this Epistle is that believers might *know* they have eternal life—assurance.

These things have I written unto you that believe on the

---

[1] *Religious Affections*, pp. 131, 137.

name of the Son of God; that ye may *know* that ye have eternal life, and that ye may believe on the name of the Son of God (I John 5:13).

Let us ask three questions about this verse: (1) To whom is John writing? "Unto you that believe." (2) What is his purpose for writing? "That ye may know. . ." (assurance). (3) How are they to know? By *"these things"* that he has written. Not by going back to the Gospel; he wrote that for a different reason, namely, that men might believe and have life through Christ.

> But these are written, that ye might believe that Jesus is the Christ, the Son of God; and that believing ye might have life through his name (John 20:31).

Well, what are these things that he has written in his little Epistle? We might call "these things" the birth marks of the second birth, or tests of eternal life. And they all have to do with Christian character and conduct, and are evidences of being born again. Therefore, Christian character and conduct have something to do with true biblical assurance: "these *things* have I written unto you that believe on the name of the Son of God; that ye may know that ye have eternal life. . . ."

Let us look at some of the birth marks of the second birth, or tests of eternal life:

First, the *test of belief* is a birth mark of the second birth. "Whosoever believeth that Jesus is the Christ is born of God. . ." (I John 5:1). That birth mark includes:

1. A belief in the Christ of the Bible as He is offered in the gospel—Prophet, Priest and King of His church.
2. A belief that reaches the whole man—his mind, his affections, and his will.
3. A belief that has been revealed and applied by the Holy Spirit in regeneration.

125

4. A belief acknowledged by the sinner in his response to the Savior.

5. A belief that is apparent in the fruits of faith and repentance.

Second, the *test of obedience* is a birth mark of the second birth: "And hereby we do know that we know him, if we keep his commandments. He that saith, I know him, and keepeth not his commandments, is a liar, and the truth is not in him. But whoso keepeth his word, in him verily is the love of God perfected: hereby know we that we are in him" (I John 2:3–5).

Bear in mind, John is not, in this passage, telling men how to be saved, or he would have told them what he did in his Gospel: "Behold the Lamb of God which taketh away the sin of the world" (John 1:29). In this passage he is talking about knowing that we have eternal life, and he is saying that obedience has something to do with knowing we are born again.

Third, the *test of love* of the brethren is a birth mark of the second birth: "We *know* that we have passed from death unto life because we love the brethren. . ." (I John 3:14); ". . . every one that loveth is born of God, and knoweth God" (I John 4:7). Love of the brethren therefore has something to do with knowing we are born again—assurance.

Fourth, the *test of the doing of righteousness* is a birth mark of the second birth: ". . . ye know that everyone that doeth righteousness is born of him." (I John 2:29). Therefore, the doing of righteousness is an evidence of the new birth and has something to do with knowing we are born again—assurance.

There are other tests of eternal life in this little Epistle, but these are sufficient to make my point, that is, that Christian character and conduct has something to do with true and full assurance and that the doctrine of assurance is vital in counseling sinners, seekers, and those who make a profession.

There are three elements to a well-grounded assurance:

1. The promises of God made real by the Spirit of God.
2. The witness of the Spirit.
3. Christian character and conduct.

To hold exclusively to the first element of assurance without the second and third is *antinomianism*. To hold exclusively to the second without the first and third is either *hypocrisy* or the *deepest self-delusion or fantasy*. To hold exclusively to the third without the first and second is *legalism*.

Let me illustrate this by three questions and their biblical answers. These three questions should concern every person who is serious about his own soul and serious in evangelizing others.

1. What is the only safe ground of a sinner's hope?
2. How does that only safe ground become the ground of my hope?
3. How am I to know that the only safe ground has become, and continues to be, the ground of my hope, so that I may be assured that my hope is not the "hope of the *hypocrite*" that shall perish, but the hope that *"maketh not ashamed"*?

Each has its own answer, and be sure not to confuse the answer of one of them for the answer of either of the others.

1. The only safe ground of the sinner's hope is the sovereign mercy of God, exercised in consistency with His righteousness, through the atoning sacrifice of His Son, made known to us in the gospel revelation.
2. The only way in which this safe ground of hope can become the ground of my hope is by believing

the Word of the truth of the gospel.

3. And the only way in which I can obtain permanent, satisfactory evidence that the only safe ground of hope has become the ground of my hope, is by continuing to believe the gospel, and by living under the influence of the gospel believed.

THE DIFFERENCE

In the area of counseling inquirers, there is a vast difference between a God-centered approach and a man-centered approach in respect to assurance. In the man-centered approach the inquirer is usually given assurance by the counselor with the use of syllogistic reasoning. For example:

Major Premise: He that believes in Christ is in the state of grace and shall be saved (John 3:16; Acts 16:31).

Minor Premise: I believe in Christ.

Conclusion: Therefore, I am saved; I have eternal life.

There is much truth in this aspect of assurance. But the question still remains, *Do I truly believe*, or do I believe as those our Lord mentioned in John 2:23, 24?: "Now when he was in Jerusalem at the passover, in the feast day, many *believed* in his name, when they saw the miracles which he did. But Jesus did not commit himself unto them, because he knew all men." They believed but were not saved because Jesus did not commit or entrust Himself to them.

In John 12:42, 43, Jesus tells us that many among the rulers believed but they would not confess him. Surely they were not saved. Again, Jesus teaches that there are those who believe for a while, but in the time of temptation fall away: "They on the rock are they, which, when they hear, receive the word with joy; and these have no root, which *for a while believe,* and in time of temptation fall away" (Luke

128

8:13). They were believers but were not saved.

Our syllogism, therefore, is not the only or conclusive truth about biblical assurance. By syllogism alone, we could prove that no one knows Christ and therefore no one is saved.

> And hereby, we do know that we know him, if we keep his commandments. He that saith, I know him, and keepeth not his commandments, is a liar, and the truth is not in him (I John 2:3, 4).

Major Premise: He that knows Christ keeps his commandments, He that says he knows Christ but does not keep his commandments is a liar.

Minor Premise: No one keeps all of Christ's commandments at all times.

Conclusion: No one knows Christ, and, therefore, no one is saved.

God-centered evangelism teaches that there is much more to true biblical assurance than a syllogism. The God-centered view of assurance is that assurance has three elements, and for a well-grounded assurance, all elements are not only important but related to each other.

In God-centered evangelism the preacher or personal worker never tries to do what only the Holy Spirit can do. The biblical view of assurance will put all preachers and personal workers out of the assurance business!

Let me now give two illustrations of the God-centered approach from that immortal volume by John Bunyan, *Pilgrim's Progress,* and an example from the life and diary of a great missionary, David Brainerd.

Evangelist speaks to a seeking sinner under conviction:

> Evangelist came to him, and asked, Wherefore dost thou cry?

He answered, Sir, I perceive by the Book in my hand, that I am condemned to die, and after that to come to Judgment; and I find that I am not willing to do the first, nor able to do the second.

Then said Evangelist, Why not willing to die, since this life is attended with so many evils? The man answered, Because I fear that this burden that is upon my back, will sink me lower than the grave; and I shall fall into Tophet. And, Sir, if I be not fit to go to prison, I am not fit to go to Judgment, and from thence to execution; and the thoughts of these things make me cry.

Then said Evangelist, If this be thy condition, Why standest thou still? He answered, Because I know not whither to go. Then he gave him a Parchment Roll, and there was written within, Fly from the Wrath to come.

The Man therefore read it, and looking upon Evangelist very carefully, said, Whither must I fly? Then said Evangelist, pointing with his finger over a very wide field, Do you see yonder Wicket Gate? The man said, No: Then said the other, Do you see yonder Shining Light? He said, I think I do. Then said Evangelist, Keep that Light in your eye, and go directly thereto, so shalt thou see the Gate; at which, when thou knockest, it shall be told thee what thou shalt do.[2]

Note several lessons from this evangelism:

1. Evangelist did not give him a one,-two,-three sales-pitch and wring a decision out of him and pronounce him saved.
2. He pointed him to the Narrow Gate.
3. He taught him to follow the light that God put on his path, and he would get more light.

[2]John Bunyan, *Pilgrim's Progress* (Banner of Truth), pp. 3, 4.

4. He did not try to play the Holy Spirit and give him assurance.

5. Later in the book Evangelist met with him to give him additional instructions.

In the second example, again, from *Pilgrim's Progress,* Hopeful was converted through Faithful's testimony in Vanity Fair. Long after his conversion, when Hopeful and Christian were a bit weary on the way, in a place called *enchanted ground,* they tried to encourage each other by sharing their testimonies. The following is part of how Faithful dealt with Hopeful, a vivid lesson in personal evangelism and an illustration of the God-centered principle of the personal worker not trying to do what only the Holy Spirit can do—give assurance.

We break in on this conversation between Christian and Hopeful. Hopeful had been telling Christian about the conviction of sin, and at this point in the conversation he begins to tell how Faithful dealt with him.

Chr. And what did you do then?

Hope. Do! I could not tell what to do, till I brake my mind to Faithful, for he and I were well acquainted, And he told me, that unless I could obtain the Righteousness of a man that never had sinned; neither mine own, nor all the Righteousness of the World could save me.

Chr. And did you think he spake true?

Hope. Had he told me so when I was pleased and satisfied with mine own amendments, I had called him Fool for his pains, but now, since I see mine own Infirmity, and the Sin that cleaves to my best performance, I have been forced to be of his opinion.

Chr. But did you think, when at first he suggested it to you, that there was such a man to be found, of whom it might justly be said, That he never com-

131

mitted Sin?

Hope. I must confess the words at first sounded strangely, but after a little more talk and company with him, I had full conviction about it.

Chr. And did you ask him, What man this was, and how you must be justified by him?

Hope. Yes, and he told me it was the Lord Jesus that dwelleth on the right hand of the Most High: And thus, said he you must be justified by him, even by trusting to what he hath done by himself in the days of his flesh, and suffered when he did hang on the Tree. I asked him further, how that Man's righteousness could be of that efficacy, as to justify another before God? And he told me, He was the Mighty God, and did what he did, and died the Death also, not for himself, but for me; to whom His doings, and the worthiness of them, should be imputed, if I believed on him.

Chr. And what did you do then?

Hope. I made my objections against my believing, for that I thought he was not willing to save me.

Chr. And what said Faithful to you then?

Hope. He bid me go to him and see; then I said it was Presumption; he said No, for I was Invited to come. Then he gave me a Book of Jesus his inditing, to encourage me the more freely to come; and he said concerning that Book, That every jot and tittle thereof stood firmer than Heaven and earth. Then I asked him what I must do when I came: And he told me, I must entreat upon my knees, with all my heart and soul, the Father to reveal him to me. Then I ask'd him further, how I must make my supplication to him? And he said, Go, and thou shalt find him upon a Mercy-Seat, where he sits all the year long, to give par-

132

don and Forgiveness to them that come. I told him, that I knew not what to say when I came. And he bid me say to this effect:

God be merciful to me a Sinner, and make me to know and believe in Jesus Christ; for I see, that if his Righteousness had not been, or I have not Faith in that Righteousness, I am utterly cast away. Lord, I have heard that thou art a merciful God, and hast ordained that thy Son Jesus Christ should be the Savior of the World; and moreover, that thou art willing to bestow upon such a poor sinner as I am, (and I am a sinner indeed) Lord, take therefore this opportunity, and magnify thy Grace in the Salvation of my soul, through thy Son Jesus Christ. Amen.

Chr. And did you do as you were bidden?

Hope. Yes; over and over, and over.

Chr. And did the Father reveal His Son to you?

Hope. Not at the first, nor second, nor third, nor fourth, nor fifth; no, nor at the sixth time neither.

Chr. What did you do then?

Hope. What! why I could not tell what to do.

Chr. Had you not thoughts of leaving off praying?

Hope. Yes; an hundred times twice told.

Chr. And what was the reason you did not?

Hope. I believed that that was true, which had been told me, to wit, That without the Righteousness of this Christ, all the World could not save me; and therefore thought I with myself, if I leave off, I die, and I can but die at the Throne of Grace. And withal this came into my mind, If it tarry, wait for it, because it will surely come, and will not tarry. So I continued Praying, until the

Father shewed me his Son.

Chr. And how was he revealed to you?

Hope. I did not see him with my bodily eyes, but with the eyes of mine Understanding; and thus it was. One day I was very sad, I think sadder than at any one time of my Life; and this sadness was through a fresh sight of the greatness and vileness of my Sins. And as I was then looking for nothing but Hell, and the everlasting Damnation of my Soul, suddenly, as I thought, I saw the Lord Jesus looking down from heaven upon me, and saying, Believe on the Lord Jesus Christ, and thou shalt be saved.

But I replied, Lord I am a great, a very great Sinner: And he answered, My Grace is sufficient for thee. Then I said, but Lord, what is Believing? And then I saw from that saying [He that cometh to me shall never hunger, and he that believeth on me shall never thirst] that Believing and Coming was all one; and that he that came, that is, ran out in his heart and affections after Salvation by Christ, he indeed believed in Christ. Then the water stood in mine eyes, and I asked further, But Lord, may such a great Sinner as I am, be indeed accepted of thee, and be saved by thee? And I heard him say, and him that cometh to me, I will in no wise cast out. Then I said, But how, Lord, must I consider of thee in my coming to thee, that my Faith may be placed aright upon thee. Then he said, Christ Jesus came into the World to save Sinners. He is the end of the Law for Righteousness to everyone that believes. He died for our Sins, and rose again for our Justification: He loved us, and washed us from our Sins in is own blood: He is mediator between

134

God and us: he ever liveth to make Intercession for us. From all which I gathered, that I must look for Righteousness in his Person, and for Satisfaction for my Sins by his Blood; that what he did in Obedience to his Father's Law, and in submitting to the Penalty thereof, was not for himself, but for him that will accept it for his Salvation, and be thankful. And now was my heart full of joy, mine eyes full of tears, and mine affections running over with love to the Name, People, and Ways of Jesus Christ.

Chr.   This was a Revelation of Christ to your soul indeed; But tell me particularly what effect this had upon your Spirit?

Hope.   It made me see that all the World, notwithstanding all the righteousness thereof, is in a state of Condemnation. It made me see that God the Father, though he be just, can justify the coming Sinner: It made me greatly ashamed of the Vileness of my former life, and confounded me with the sense of mine own Ignorance; for there never came thought into my heart before now, that showed me so the beauty of Jesus Christ: It made me love a Holy Life, and long to do something for the honour and glory of the name of the Lord Jesus; Yea, I thought that had I now a thousand gallons of blood in my body, I could spill it all for the sake of the Lord Jesus.[3]

Again, note, there is the absence of salesmanship—no decisionism—and Faithful does not try to play the Holy Spirit and give assurance.

Now, let us see this same principle from the life of that great missionary, David Brainerd:

---

[3]John Bunyan, *Pilgrim's Progress* (Banner of Truth), pp. 161-65.

July 2. Was obliged to leave these Indians at Cross-weksung, thinking it my duty, as soon as health would admit, again to visit those at the Forks of Delaware. When I came to take leave of them, and spoke something particulary to each of them, they all earnestly inquired when I would come again, and expressed a great desire of being further instructed. And of their own accord agreed, that when I should come again, they would all meet and live together during my continuance with them; and that they would do their utmost endeavors to gather all the other Indians in these parts that were yet further remote. And when I parted, one told me with many tears, "She wished God would change her heart"; another, that "she wanted to find Christ": and an old man that had been one of their chiefs, wept bitterly with concern for his soul. I then promised them to return as speedily as my health and business elsewhere would admit, and felt not a little concerned at parting, lest the good impressions then apparent upon numbers of them, might decline and wear off, when the means came to cease; and yet could not but hope that He who, I trusted, had begun a good work among them, and who I knew did not stand in need of means to carry it on, would maintain and promote it.

At the same time, I must confess that I had often seen encouraging appearances among the Indians elsewhere prove wholly abortive; and it appeared the favor would be so great, if God should now after I had passed through so considerable a series of almost fruitless labors and fatigues, and after my rising hopes had been so often frustrated among these poor pagans, give me any special success in my labors with them. I could not believe, and scarce dared to hope that the event would be so happy, scarce ever found myself more suspended between hope and fear, in any affair, or at any time, than this.

This encouraging disposition and readiness to receive instruction, now apparent among these Indians, seems to have been the happy effect of the conviction that one or two of them met with some time since at the Forks of Delaware, who have since endeavored to show their friends the evil of idolatry. And although the other Indians seemed but little to regard, but rather to deride them, yet this, perhaps, has put them into a thinking posture of mind, or at least, given them some thoughts about Christianity, and excited in some of them a curiosity to hear, and so made way for the present encouraging attention. An apprehension that this might be the case here, has given me encouragement that God may in such a manner bless the means I have used with Indians in other places, where there is as yet no appearance of it. If so, may His name have the glory of it; for I have learned by experience that He only can open the ear, engage the attention, and incline the heart of poor benighted, prejudiced pagans to receive instruction.[4]

It is important that every serious person who seeks to evangelize *must* study the biblical view of assurance as it relates to counseling and evangelizing.[5]

---

[4]By Jonathan Edwards, *The Life and Diary of David Brainerd*.

[5]Recommended material on assurance: Westminster Confession of Faith, Chapter 18; Baptist Confession of 1689 (London Confession), Chapter 18; *Heaven on Earth*, by Thomas Brooks; *The Christian's Great Interest*, by William Guthrie.

13. CONCLUSION

It is generally recognized by discerning Christians that sound doctrine is on the wane, and yet many of the Lord's people take comfort from supposing that the gospel is still being widely preached and that large numbers are being saved. Alas! their optimism is ill-founded. When the evangelistic message now being delivered and printed is scrutinized, when *"modern evangelism"* is weighed in the balance of Holy Writ, it is found wanting and lacking in that which is vital to genuine conversion, lacking in that which will produce transformed lives, new creatures in Christ.

Most evangelism of this day is not only superficial, but radically defective. It is utterly lacking a foundation on which to base an appeal for sinners to come to Christ. There is a lamentable lack of proportion (the mercy of God made far more prominent than His holiness, His love more than His wrath), and there is a fatal omission of that which God has given for the purpose of imparting a knowledge of sin. There is not only the introduction of *bright singing, humorous witticisms, entertaining anecdotes, high pressured techniques, excesses, and commercialism,* but there is a *studied* omission of the dark background upon which the gospel can effectually shine forth. But this is only the negative side of that which is lacking. Worse still, is that which is being retailed by much of the evangelism of our day. The *positive content* of the message is nothing but throwing dust in the sinner's eyes. Many times his soul is put to sleep by the devil's opiate, ministered in a most unsuspected form. Those who have been the recipients of the message being delivered from many pulpits and platforms today are being fatally deceived. Modern evangelism has lost its grip on the biblical *gospel* message. Although many serious Christians do not appreciate the resulting fruit of this man-centered message, they do not seem to understand that the root of the problem is the message itself. The new message fails to produce:

1. Deep reverence for the God of the Bible.
2. Deep repentance and humility.
3. A real spirit of worship.
4. A proper love and concern for the church.

Because it is man-centered, it fails to make man God-centered in his thoughts and God-fearing in his heart. Since it does not begin with God, it is not designed to make man God-centered.

The God-centered message is essentially the proclamation of a God who is sovereign in mercy and judgment, sovereign in creation and redemption—the mighty Lord on whom man depends for all good, both in nature and grace. To put it another way, the God-centered message is *God* and His way with man. The subject of the man-centered message is *man* and the things God does for him, or the help God gives him.

It is the sincere purpose of this book to encourage God-centered evangelism. Some who read this book will agree with the doctrinal substance and yet not seem to demonstrate the real zeal for carrying out our Lord's clear command, *"Go ye"*: ". . . as my Father hast sent me, even so send I you" (John 20:21); "But ye shall receive power, after that the Holy Ghost is come upon you: and ye shall be witnesses unto me both in Jerusalem, and in all Judaea, and in Samaria, and unto the uttermost part of the earth" (Acts 1:8). It must be pressed upon this group that the same Bible that teaches us *who* does the saving, also teaches us *how* He does it, that is, the means God uses in bringing the sheep into the fold or the fish into the gospel net.

Others who will read this book are among those who have zeal and do actually seek to carry out our Lord's heavenly mandate, but do not have a sound doctrinal foundation, and do not seem to know what God taught Jonah: ". . . salvation is of the LORD" (Jonah 2:9). This group does not see that many of the failures of their evangelism to produce true conversion are due to the lack of biblical content in the message and the carnal methods employed in evangelism.

The following letter is a yet living Christian mother's actual confession, which could be duplicated ten thousand times. This letter illustrates the typical error of evangelistic zeal without doctrinal understanding. Note well, "*I pressed him into a decision.*"

A CHRISTIAN MOTHER'S CONFESSION

When I saw my son going deeper and deeper into crime and rebellion of every kind, I became so anxious for his soul to be saved — thus delivered from evil — I pressed him into a "decision for Christ." He said the "sinner's prayer," but his life style unto this present time has not changed, but now he is bitter towards God for he says, "God let him down."

The gospel will not fail because its success does not depend on man or his methods. Its success depends on the wisdom, mercy, and power of God. Jesus said, ". . . I will build my church. . ." (Matt. 16:18).

I want to close with a note of encouragement to evangelize, regarding *the joy of seeing Christ change hearts, lives, homes, and destinations.* Apart from my own salvation the greatest joy I have ever known in this world is being the *means of taking the gospel to some poor lost sinner and seeing God magnify His grace in the salvation of lost souls through the power of that gospel to make a saving change.*

This is illustrated in the parable of the man who found his

lost sheep: ". . . he calleth together his friends and neighbours, saying unto them, Rejoice with me; for I have found my sheep which was lost. I say unto you, that likewise joy shall be in heaven over one sinner that repenteth" (Luke 15:6, 7). This joy and rejoicing is the result of seeing the lost sheep found—through evangelizing.

John G. Paton, a great missionary, saw the harvest of sacrificial labor in a gracious work of conversion in the New Hebrides. He tells of his first communion service, when he put the bread and wine into those dark hands, once stained with the blood of cannibalism, now reaching forth to receive the emblem of the blood of Christ. "I had a foretaste of the joy of glory that well nigh brake my heart to pieces. I shall never taste a deeper bliss till I gaze on the glorified face of Jesus Himself."

The following is a paraphrase of I Corinthians, chapter 13, by Dr. Joseph Clark:

THE GREATEST OF THESE IS EVANGELISM

Though I speak with the tongues of scholarship, and though I use approved methods of education, and fail to win others to Christ, or to build them up in Christian character, I am become as the moan of the wind in a Syrian desert.

And though I have the best of methods and understand all mysteries of religious psychology, and though I have all biblical knowledge, and lose not myself in the task of winning others to Christ, I become as a cloud of mist in an open sea.

And though I read all Sunday School literature, and attend Sunday School conventions, and institutes and summer school, and yet am satisfied with less than winning souls to Christ and establishing others in Christian character and service, it profiteth nothing.

The soul-winning servant, the character-building servant, suffereth long and is kind; he envieth not others who are free from the servant's task; he vaunteth not himself, is not puffed up with intellectual pride.

Such a servant doth not behave himself unseemly between Sundays, seeketh not his own comfort, is not easily provoked. Beareth all things, believeth all things, hopeth all things.

And now abideth knowledge, methods, the Message, these three: but the greatest of these is the Message.

Jesus said:

. . . Go ye into all the world, and preach the gospel to every creature. . . ."

And ye are witnesses of these things.

. . . as my Father hath sent me, even so send I you.

But ye shall receive power, after that the Holy Ghost is come upon you: and ye shall be witnesses unto me both in Jerusalem, and in all Judaea, and in Samaria, and unto the uttermost part of the earth.

APPENDIX:
THE NATURE OF SAVING FAITH

Just over four hundred years ago, late in October, a young Augustinian monk, professor of theology and pastor in Wittenberg, Germany, in the fire of his zeal for Christian truth, nailed 95 theses to the door of the Castle Church. He had left the study of law and entered the priesthood, seeking to be justified before God. His name was Martin Luther. As a result of studying the Scriptures, he discovered biblical truths that had long been covered and obscured by the ritual and rubble of Rome. One of the great truths then restored to the church was justification by faith alone.

The issue before us today is not a denial of justification by faith alone, but rather a perversion of that doctrine. Present-day preaching often excludes the possibility of spurious faith; however, religious deception is the worst kind of deception because of its eternal consequences. We must distinguish properly between justifying faith and spurious or counterfeit faith.

The Bible very clearly warns against spurious faith; therefore, I wish to direct attention to its warnings and note some differences between spurious and true believers. I intend to cite biblical cases of spurious faith, showing that the Scriptures teach the existence of belief which is not saving faith. I propose also to define true faith and give biblical examples of that faith which savingly joins one to Jesus Christ for all eternity.

SPURIOUS OR COUNTERFEIT FAITH

The Bible teaches that there is a spurious faith. In the parable of the sower, Jesus spoke of *temporary faith.* "They on the rock are they, which, when they hear, receive the word with joy; and these have no root, which for a while *believe*, and in time of temptation fall away" (Luke 8:13). These believers received the word with joy and believed for a season; but in the time of trial, they fell away. They lacked root and fruit; and they did not continue.

Paul spoke of "Believing in vain" (I Cor. 15:2). This is non-saving faith. Though it has many marks of true saving faith, the evidence of temporary faith soon appears. It lacks the following characteristics of saving faith: (1) continuance in trusting Christ, and in devotion to Him and His service; (2) desire to be useful in Christ's church; (3) attendance to Christian duty; (4) love of prayer and the Word of God and of assembling with God's people in worship; (5) devotion to loving the people of God as such; (6) progress in knowledge of self, sin, and the Savior; (7) progress in loving holiness and hating sin, with increased conviction of and humility concerning personal sinfulness.

A very vivid example of spurious faith is the case of Simon Magus. Of him it is written, "Then Simon himself *believed* also: and when he was baptized, he continued with Philip" (Acts 8:13). He expressed such faith that Philip took him to be a genuine Christian and admitted him to Christian privileges. Yet Peter later told Simon that he would perish with his money, warning him, "Thou hast neither part nor lot in this matter: for thy heart is not right in the sight of God. . . . I perceive that thou art in the gall of bitterness, and in the bond of iniquity" (Acts 8:20–23).

A man may believe *all* the truth contained in Scripture, as far as he is acquainted with it; indeed, he may be familiar with far more truth than many genuine Christians. And as his knowledge may be more extensive, so his faith may be more comprehensive. He may go even as far as Paul had. Although Paul believed all the Scripture before his conversion, his faith was not saving faith. Note also Agrippa. "King Agrippa, believest thou the prophets? I know that thou *believest*" (Acts 26:27). But this faith did not save him.

James speaks of *dead* faith (James 2:17, 26), the giving of mere mental assent to certain historical facts. He also speaks of *devils'* faith (James 2:19). This is a religious appropriation of these facts. The demons have a sound confession. They believe in the person ("Jesus, thou Son of God") and the power ("art thou come to torment us?") of Christ (Matt. 8:29).

It is indeed searching and solemn to discover how much the Bible speaks of unsaved people having faith in the Lord. Though it seems incredible, there are those willing to have Christ as their Savior, yet who are most reluctant to submit to Him as their Lord, to be at His command, and to be governed by His laws. But more shocking still, there are unregenerate persons who profess Christ as Lord, and yet are not in possession of saving faith. The scriptural proof of this assertion is found in Matthew 7:22, 23: 'Many will say to me in that day, Lord, Lord, have we not prophesied in Thy name? and in Thy name cast out demons? and in Thy name done many wonderful works? and then will I profess unto them, I never knew you: depart from me, ye that work iniquity." Here is a large class (many) who profess subjection to Christ as Lord, who do many mighty works in His name, and thus can even show you their faith by their works, and yet theirs is not saving faith. "Depart from me," said Jesus.

It is impossible to say how far non-saving faith may go or how close it may resemble true saving faith. Saving faith has Christ as its object; so has spurious faith. "Many believed in his name, when they saw the miracles which he did. But Jesus did not commit himself unto them, because he knew all men'' (John 2:23, 24). Saving faith is wrought by the Holy Spirit; so also spurious faith has an apparent spirituality and may even partake to some degree of illuminating grace (Heb. 6:4). Saving faith is a receiving of the Word of God; so also is spurious faith. ''He that receiveth the seed into stony places . . . heareth the word, and anon with joy *receiveth* it; yet hath he not root in himself, but dureth for a while'' (Matt. 13:20, 21). Saving faith will cause a man to prepare for the coming of the Lord; so will spurious faith. Both the foolish and the wise virgins had the lamp of profession—they all *trimmed their lamps* and said ''Lord, Lord''—but half heard the answer, ''I know you not'' (Matt. 25:1-13). Saving faith is accompanied with joy; so is spurious faith. ''They on the rock . . . receive the word with *joy*'' (Luke 8:13).

When we realize how far spurious faith can go in its counterfeits, we are prone to say, ''All this is very unsettling and confusing.'' Yes, it is distressing! But, if we value our souls or care for the souls of others, we will not dismiss this subject lightly. Since the Bible teaches that there is a faith in Christ which does not save and that it is easy to be deceived, we must earnestly seek the help of the Spirit. The Spirit Himself cautions us at this very point. ''A deceived heart hath turned him aside'' (Isa. 44:20). ''The pride of thine heart hath deceived thee'' (Obad. 3). ''Take heed that ye be not deceived'' (Luke 21:8).

Satan uses his cunning and power most tenaciously and successfully in convincing people that they have saving faith when they do not. He deceives more souls by this stratagem than by all other devices combined. How many Satanblinded souls will read this and say, ''It does not apply to me; I know that my faith is genuine.'' Satan dissuades many from heeding that most salutary exhortation: ''Examine yourselves, whether ye be in the faith; prove your own selves'' (II Cor. 13:5).

Our Lord's parables show that He continually warned against self-deception. Spiritual houses often look the same until the storm of God's judgment comes (Matt. 7:24–27). Then it is revealed that one house is spurious (built on sand) and one is genuine (built on rock). Wheat and tares look so much alike that only the Lord Himself can separate them (Matt. 13:24–30).

Failure to recognize the Bible's teaching on counterfeit faith has led to other errors. The tendency is to treat spurious believers as saved but not consecrated or filled with the Spirit. The folly is often compounded by calling those who give no Bible evidence of saving faith *carnal Christians*, since they do not act like Christians. The solution to this unbiblical dilemma is sought in some kinds of second experience or second work of grace. Thus there is constant appeal to the *carnal Christian,* who in reality is a spurious believer, to finally surrender to Christ's lordship and be filled with (even baptized in) the Spirit.

The great theologians of the past recognized that the Bible distinguishes between spurious faith and saving faith. Charles Hodge speaks of *historical* or *speculative* faith, *temporary* faith, and *saving* faith (*Systematic Theology* 3:67–68). James P. Boyce, one of the greatest Southern Baptist theologians and principal founder of their first seminary, speaks of *implicit* faith, *historical* faith, *temporary* or *delusive* faith, and *saving* faith (*Abstract of Systematic Theology,* pp. 389-94). With these great men of God, we hold tenaciously to that great hopeful and liberating truth of the Bible—justification by faith alone. But we also recognize that faith which is alone is not the faith which justifies.

TRUE SAVING FAITH DESCRIBED

Regeneration is inseparable from its effects, one of which is saving faith. Without regeneration it is morally and spiritually impossible to savingly believe in Christ. Except a man be born again, he cannot see, he cannot understand, he cannot come to Christ (John 3:3; 6:37, 44; I Cor. 2:14). Regeneration is the renewing of the heart and mind; and the renewed heart and mind must act according to their nature.

Regeneration is the act of God alone. But faith is not the act of God. It is not God who believes in Christ for salvation; it is the sinner. Although it is by God's grace alone that a person is able to believe, faith is an activity of the person alone. In saving faith we receive and rest upon Christ alone for salvation. True, this is a strange, and to some extent, undefinable mixture. But this is precisely what the Bible teaches. This is God's way of salvation, expressing His supreme wisdom, power, and grace.

THE ACTING OF TRUE SAVING FAITH

True justifying faith is, in the Lord's deep wisdom and condescension, variously expressed in Scripture according to its different actings toward God and its outgoings after Him. True faith is sometimes spoken of as a desire for union with God in Christ—as a *willing*. "And whosoever will, let him take the water of life freely" (Rev. 22:17). Scripture also speaks of *looking* to Him. "Look unto me and be ye saved, all the ends of the earth" (Isa. 45:22; this text was used of God in Spurgeon's conversion). This may be the weakest act of faith. True faith is also expressed as *"hungering* and *thirsting* after righteousness" (Matt. 5:6).

True faith sometimes goes out in the act of *leaning* on the Lord; the soul taking up Christ as a resting-stone because God has so offered Christ. Though He may be a stumbling-stone and a rock of offense to others, true faith is not ashamed of Him (Rom. 9:33). The acting of true faith is sometimes expressed in Scripture as *trusting* and *staying* on God. He keeps in perfect peace those whose minds are *stayed* on Him; such do *trust* in Him. *Trust* in the Lord, for

150

with Him is everlasting strength (Isa. 26:3, 4). They that *trust* in the Lord shall be as Mount Zion, which abides forever (Ps. 125:1). The Lord has made promises to this way of faith's acting, knowing that in this way true faith often goes out after Him.

True faith embraces Christ in whatever way the Scripture holds Him out to poor sinners. To the *naked* soul, destitute of a covering to keep it from the storm of God's wrath, Christ is *fine raiment* (Rev. 3:17, 18). Accordingly, faith's work here is to "put on the Lord Jesus" (Rom. 13:14). To the soul that is *hungry* and *thirsty* for something that will everlastingly satisfy, Christ Jesus is *"milk, wine, water, the bread of life, and the true manna"* (Isa. 55:1, 2; John 6:48, 51). True faith will *"go, buy, eat, and drink abundantly"* (Isa. 55:1; John 6:53, 57). To the soul that is *pursued for guilt* and is not able to withstand the charge, Christ Jesus is the *city of refuge*. The poor guilty man exercises true faith by fleeing to Christ for refuge, laying hold on the hope set before him (Heb. 6:18).

In a word, whatever way Christ may benefit poor sinners, He declares Himself able to do. True faith desires Christ in whatever way He holds Himself out in the Scriptures. If He is held out as a *Bridegroom,* true faith goes out to Him as a *bride.* If He is held out as a *Father* (Isa. 9:6), true faith takes the place of a child. If He is held out as a *Shepherd,* true faith takes the place of a *sheep.* If He is set forth as *Lord,* true faith acknowledges Him to be the *Sovereign.* True faith desires Christ and aspires to be conformed to His image.

It is important to remember, in considering the actings of true saving faith, that every true believer does not manifest all these various actings and exercises of faith, for their condition does not require them. Not everyone in the New Testament is told to sell his possessions (Mark 10:21). Surely, not everyone dares say, "though he slay me, yet will I trust him" (Job 13:15). Many would not have pursued

Christ like the woman of Canaan (Matt. 15:22–28) but in discouragement would have given up.

There is, however, one thing common to all who possess true saving faith; that is, a heart-satisfaction with God's plan of salvation by Christ. When one is pleased with God's method of satisfying His justice through Christ's person and work and when the soul and heart embrace that plan, then one is believing unto salvation.

Saving faith is not a difficult, mysterious, hardly attainable thing. We must first acknowledge it to be God's gift, above the power of flesh and blood. God must draw men to Christ. "No man can come to me, except the Father which hath sent me draw him" (John 6:44). "For unto you it is given in the behalf of Christ . . . to believe on him" (Phil. 1:29).

Shall that which consists much in *desire* be judged a mysterious, difficult thing? If men have but a true appetite, they have a mark of true saving faith. They are "blessed that hunger after righteousness" (Matt. 5:6). If you desire, you are welcome (Rev. 22:17). Is it a matter of such intricacy and difficulty earnestly to *look* to the exalted Savior (Isa. 45:22)? Is it mysterious or difficult to receive that which is sincerely offered and declared to be mine if I will but accept it? "Open thy mouth wide, and I will fill it" (Ps. 81:10). Such is justifying faith.

"It was the glory of our Protestant Reformation to discover again the purity of the evangel. The Reformers recognized that the essence of saving faith is to bring the sinner lost and dead in trespasses and sins into direct personal contact with the Saviour himself, contact which is nothing less than that of self-commitment to him in all the glory of his person and perfection of his work as he is freely and fully offered in the gospel" (John Murray, *Redemption: Accomplished and Applied,* p. 112). Here, Professor Murray gives us a superb definition of justifying and saving faith.

This is the faith of God's elect, and by it they are able to believe to the saving of their souls. This faith is the work of the Spirit in their hearts and is ordinarily wrought by the ministry of the Word. By this kind of faith, God's sheep hear His Word and believe to be true all that is revealed in the Scriptures. Where this faith is, there is a yielding of obedience to the commands, a trembling at the threatenings, and an embracing of the promises of God for this life and the life to come. The principal acts of saving faith are accepting, receiving, and resting upon Christ alone for justification, sanctification, and eternal life. Justifying faith, therefore, includes *knowledge, conviction,* and *trust.*

DIFFERENCES BETWEEN SPURIOUS AND TRUE FAITH

There is a hope that shall perish (Job 8:13, 14) and a hope that makes not ashamed (Rom. 5:5). Likewise, there is a faith which saves and a faith which damns. The need to distinguish between the two is vital on the contemporary church scene. "There is a generation that are pure in their own eyes, and *yet* is not washed from their filthiness" (Prov. 30:12). "There is a way which seemeth right unto a man, *but* the end thereof are the ways of death" (Prov. 14:12). These searching passages have a very real application to our church membership today.

This brings us to our last consideration; that is, the differences between spurious faith and justifying faith, or false believers and true believers. There are many differences, but I point out four that separate the wheat from the chaff, the genuine from the counterfeit.

The first difference is that spurious believers want Christ, but *not without exception.* They want the grace of Christ, but not the government of Christ—like the prodigal son who wanted his father's goods but not his father's government. They desire the benefits of the cross without bowing to the implications of the crown. They want to go to heaven, but not by the narrow way that leads there. They desire the free gift of eternal life, but will not receive it with empty hands. Yes, they want Christ, but not without exception. They want Christ and their other lovers also. They want to be saved from the consequences of sin, but not from sin itself. But our Lord came to save from sin. This is clear from the very first chapter of the New Testament. "Thou shalt call his name Jesus: for he shall save his people from their *sins*" (Matt. 1:21). Jesus is not just a hell insurance policy, but a Savior from sin and its consequences.

True saving faith wants Christ *without exception*. This is illustrated by our Lord's parables in Matthew 13. "The kingdom of heaven is like unto treasure hid in a field; the which when a man hath found, he hideth and for joy thereof goeth and selleth all that he hath, and buyeth that field" (Matt. 13:44). "Again, the kingdom of heaven is like unto a merchant man, seeking goodly pearls: who, when he had found one pearl of great price, went and sold all that he had, and bought it" (Matt. 13:45, 46). The treasure and the pearl is Christ; and saving faith wants *Him without exception*.

The second difference between spurious believers and true believers is that true faith wants Christ as He is offered in the Scriptures; that is, as the only Mediator between God and man (I Tim. 2:5). As Mediator, Christ has three offices: Prophet, Priest, and King of His church. First, as Priest, Christ procures pardon and peace by His sacrifice on the cross and maintains peace by His intercession. Second, as Prophet, Christ is wisdom—teacher and counselor in all things. Third, as anointed King, Christ rules and reigns over the true believer in all things and protects him from all his enemies.

Spurious believers want Christ only as a Priest to procure pardon and peace, but not as a Prophet to instruct them or as a King to rule over them. We are not saved, however, by one of the offices of Christ, but by *Him*. "He that hath the Son hath life" (I John 5:12). If we have *Him*, we must have Him *in all of His offices.*

The third difference is that spurious believers never close with Christ and all the inconveniences that follow. They want Christ but have never done what Jesus commanded— that is, counted the cost (Luke 14:25-33). Every serious Christian knows that the Christian life is not a gospel hay ride. All is not "happy, happy, happy" or "jolly, jolly, jolly." The language of the Christian life is also "I war," "I fight," "I wrestle." Jesus was honest about this. Any serious study of Luke 9 and 14 will underscore just how honest at the outset Jesus was in His dealings with men.

True faith wants Christ and all the inconveniences that follow. It costs to be a Christian. I am not talking about the price of redemption. That is infinite. We are redeemed with the precious blood of Christ. I am talking about what it costs to live a Christian life. It costs you nothing to *become* a Christian; but it may cost you everything to *be* a Christian.

The fourth difference between spurious and true believers is that the spurious believer's heart is not changed, and, therefore, his faith is not operative. Simon Magus *believed,* but his heart was not right in the sight of God (Acts 8:13, 21). True faith is operative, purifying the heart (Acts 15:8, 9).

In summary: (1) Saving faith wants Christ without exception. (2) Saving faith receives Christ in all of His offices—as Prophet, Priest, and King. (3) Saving faith receives Christ and all the inconveniences that follow. (4) Saving faith is operative, purifying the heart. None of these things is true of spurious faith.

We must distinguish properly between justifying faith and spurious faith. The consequences of remaining in deception are too enormous to neglect self-examination. There is a faith which will not save and men must be warned of its fatal consequences. We are justified by faith alone, but true faith has distinguishing traits. That faith which is alone is not the kind of faith which justifies.

For I am not ashamed of the gospel of Christ: for it is the power of God unto salvation to every one that believeth; to the Jew first, and also to the Greek. For therein is the righteousness of God revealed from faith to faith: as it is written, The just shall live by faith (Romans 1:16, 17).

Books on Evangelism Highly Recommended:

Walter Chantry, *Today's Gospel: Authentic or Synthetic?* (Banner of Truth Trust).

J. I. Packer, *Evangelism and the Sovereignty of God* (Inter-Varsity Press).

Will Metzger, *Tell the Truth* (InterVarsity Press).

C. John Miller, *Evangelism and Your Church* (Presbyterian and Reformed Publishing Company).